THE CONSTITUTIONAL DOCTRINES
OF JUSTICE HARLAN

BY

FLOYD BARZILIA CLARK, Ph.D.
Assistant Professor of Political Science in Pennsylvania State College

THE LAWBOOK EXCHANGE, LTD.
Clark, New Jersey

ISBN 978-1-58477-446-4

Lawbook Exchange edition 2004, 2019

The quality of this reprint is equivalent to the quality of the original work.

THE LAWBOOK EXCHANGE, LTD.
33 Terminal Avenue
Clark, New Jersey 07066-1321

*Please see our website for a selection of our other publications
and fine facsimile reprints of classic works of legal history:*
www.lawbookexchange.com

Library of Congress Cataloging-in-Publication Data

Clark, Floyd Barzilia, b. 1886.
   The constitutional doctrines of Justice Harlan / by Floyd Barzilia Clark.
     p. cm.
   Originally published: Baltimore : Johns Hopkins Press, 1915.
   ISBN 1-58477-446-0 (cloth: alk. paper)
   1. Constitutional Law--United States. 2. Harlan, John Marshall, 1833-
1911. I. Harlan, John Marshall, 1833-1911. II. Title.

KF4550.Z9C52 2004
342.73—dc22   2004040731

Printed in the United States of America on acid-free paper

THE CONSTITUTIONAL DOCTRINES
OF JUSTICE HARLAN

BY

FLOYD BARZILIA CLARK, Ph.D.
Assistant Professor of Political Science in Pennsylvania State College

BALTIMORE
THE JOHNS HOPKINS PRESS
1915

PRESS OF
THE NEW ERA PRINTING COMPANY
LANCASTER, PA.

TABLE OF CONTENTS

PREFACE

Two temptations assail writers of biographies, or of studies of a similar kind,—to overestimate or to underestimate. It is hard for the student of a man's career to see both sides, and after giving due consideration to each, to form a fair judgment. Throughout this study I have been aware of these two dangers, but I am not sure that in all respects they have been avoided.

It needs to be emphasized that in studying the constitutional doctrines of a single great judge as found in his dissenting opinions, the prevailing opinions of the court must of necessity appear at their worst, for the criticisms of the minority are of course directed at the weak points in the reasoning of the majority. In so far, then, as I have accepted Justice Harlan's arguments and found unconvincing the rulings of the Supreme Court, it must be remembered that I am criticising only the weaker points of a few decisions of that great tribunal.

This study was prepared partly at the Summer School of Columbia University, but principally in the Department of Political Science of the Johns Hopkins University. I wish to express my gratitude for suggestions made by Mr. A. M. Groves, a graduate student of this University, who read the manuscript before it went to press; I owe to Professor T. R. Powell, of New York, my knowledge of many of the basic principles of constitutional law; but the study was prepared under the direction of Dr. W. W. Willoughby, of the Johns Hopkins University, without whose aid its production would not have been possible.

F. B. C.

TABLE OF CASES

TABLE OF CASES

THE CONSTITUTIONAL DOCTRINES OF
JUSTICE HARLAN

INTRODUCTION

John Marshall Harlan was born on June 1, 1833, in Boyle
County, Kentucky. His father, the Honorable James Harlan, was an active lawyer of that State, and christened his
son for the judgeship, giving him the name John Marshall
in honor of that highly respected formulator of the principles of our constitutional law. The subject of our study
grew up at a time when the air was hot with abolition sentiment, and in a State where opinion was sharply divided.
Though his father was not an abolitionist, he was an eman-
cipator, and some time before the war he set his slaves free.
The young Harlan imbibed this spirit of emancipation, and
when the test came he espoused the cause of freedom. He
and his father fought valiantly to turn the tide of opinion
in Kentucky against secession, and were influential in
preventing that State from joining the Confederacy. When
Kentucky refused to furnish its quota of soldiers to the
Union, Harlan was one of those who volunteered to
fight on the northern side. He organized a regiment of
militia, and led them in battle against the South. He was
thus, to start with, colonel of the Tenth Kentucky Infantry,
but he rose rapidly in rank, and in 1863 was acting-com-
mander of a brigade. At this time, however, the death of
his father made it necessary, for family reasons, that he return to civil life. At the time of his resignation from the
army his name had just been sent by Mr. Lincoln to the
Senate as a full brigadier-general, but his services in the
army were ended. He remained loyal to the northern
cause throughout his career, and many times asserted his
disapproval of the deprivation of the rights which the

negroes were supposed to have obtained by the new amendments to the Constitution of the United States.

Mr. Harlan received his education at Centre College, Kentucky, where he received the degree of A.B. in 1850, and at Transylvania University, where he studied law. The degree of LL.D. was conferred on him by the following institutions: Bowdoin in 1883, Centre College and Princeton in 1884, and the University of Pennsylvania in 1900. From 1889 to his death in 1911 he was professor of constitutional law at the George Washington University, in Washington, D. C.

He married Miss Malvina F. Shanklin, of Evansville, Indiana, December 23, 1856, and had a long and happy married life. His three sons, Dr. Richard Davenport Harlan, the Honorable James S. Harlan, and Mr. John Maynard Harlan, occupy prominent positions in the service of the nation. The oldest, Dr. Richard Davenport Harlan, holds a high position as an educator, the second is a member of the Interstate Commerce Commission, and the youngest is an attorney-at-law in Chicago.

Before and during his service as associate justice of the Supreme Court, Mr. Harlan held responsible appointments outside of his regular service as judge. He was twice candidate for the governorship of Kentucky, and was attorney-general of that State from 1863 to 1867. His entrance into national affairs was marked by the part which he took in the Cincinnati Republican Convention of 1876, which nominated Mr. Hayes as Republican candidate for the presidency. In this convention he was leader of the forces for the nomination of General B. H. Bristow, a member of Grant's Cabinet; but when Bristow's nomination became impossible, his supporters united with others for the nomination of Mr. Hayes. When Hayes was elected to the presidency, he wished to appoint a representative lawyer from Kentucky as one of his Cabinet and offered the attorney-generalship to Mr. Harlan, who, however, did not see his way clear to accept.

Mr. Harlan's appointment by President Hayes upon the

so-called Louisiana Commission was a notable incident in his career. The purpose of the commission was to aid in the settlement of an election dispute in Louisiana. This commission must of course be distinguished from the state Returning Board which had been appointed at an earlier date to examine election returns in that State. The Returning Board had given the state vote to Hayes in the national election, and had likewise turned the governorship of the State over to the Republican candidate. The Republicans wished to get the support of the national army to secure them in power, and appealed to Hayes to this end. To clear up the situation the Louisiana Commission was appointed. The members of the commission, being appointed by the President and reporting only to him, had no powers, but were to hear the complaints of both sides and to serve as a safety valve to the pent-up grievances. They soon found that the return of the federal army to the State was unwise. Owing to the fact that the property owners voluntarily sent in their taxes to the Democratic organization, its opponents soon disbanded for lack of funds, and the situation settled itself. The commission was doubtless influential in helping to undo some of the crooked work of the Returning Board. It was an honor to have been upon a board, the majority of whose members were Republicans, which was honest enough to recommend that the Democratic government be upheld at a time when one would not have expected such a recommendation. Mr. Harlan's sense of honor must have helped greatly in maintaining the integrity of the commission.

Mr. Harlan also served as one of the American arbitrators on the Behring Sea Tribunal, which met in Paris in 1893 to settle the dispute between the United States and England over the Alaskan seal fisheries. An eyewitness said of his appearance on this occasion: "I can never forget a scene I once witnessed in Paris, when the Behring Sea Arbitration Tribunal was sitting there, with John Marshall Harlan of Kentucky, at one end of the court and John

Tyler Morgan of Alabama at the other. Both were then in the Indian Summer of their manhood—Harlan with his noble and matchless form, the God-gifted Morgan, with his beautiful face and head that sculptors and painters might have loved to copy. My heart swelled with pride as I looked upon those two great American citizens, who had been opposing generals in the Civil War, and fancied that I saw in them reproductions of Brutus and Cicero."[1]

Mr. Harlan was simple and childlike in his daily conduct, fond of home, and of his home people and relatives. He was deeply religious in his nature. He honored the Constitution of the United States, and the Bible seemed to be the only thing that he placed above it. "The Constitution and the Bible were the objects of his constant thought and consideration, and if the latter was to him always vox Dei, the former, vox populi, was no less so."[2]

He deeply loved his State as well as his nation. "I remember when the case of Taylor v. Beckham was argued in this court. At that time intense feeling existed in Kentucky. It was indeed a period that tried men's souls as well as appealed to the sound judgment of the people of our State. During the argument the sympathies of Justice Harlan were so awakened that he shed tears."[3]

Mr. Harlan was associate justice of the Supreme Court of the United States for nearly thirty-four years, from December 10, 1877, until his death on October 14, 1911. Though he was appointed by President Hayes immediately after his return from service on the Louisiana Commission, there was nothing in that experience that would speak for political reward. Furthermore, his whole career shows that he would not have accepted an appointment merely for political reasons.

His term of service was exceeded in length by only two

---

[1] Remarks of Mr. Hannis Taylor in Proceedings of the Bar and Officers of the Supreme Court of the United States in Memory of John Marshall Harlan, Dec. 16, 1911. P. 30.
[2] Remarks of Attorney-General Wickersham, in ibid., p. 45.
[3] Remarks of William Bradley, in ibid., p. 27.

justices,—Marshall and Field, in each case by less than a
year. His labors were not surpassed, however, by these
men of longer service. Something more than seven hundred
decisions wherein he spoke for the majority bear his name,
and his dissenting and concurring opinions pass the hundred
mark.

While a justice he was more than a judge. His interest
went further than a contemplation of the arguments bearing on the cases, and he thought deeply outside of questions
of constitutional importance, although he was reluctant to
express his opinion upon great issues likely to be brought before the court. In a letter to a young friend, written August
12, 1911, only two months before he died, he made the following comments in reference to the conditions under which
new States should be admitted into the Union: "I hope
that the President will put his feet down firmly upon the
recall of judges in Arizona and New Mexico, while in territorial condition. It is one thing for these people, *after
becoming States,* to amend their constitutions, and provide
for the recall of judges. It is quite a different thing for Congress to give its *sanction* to the principle of the 'recall' by
admitting these Territories into the Union with constitutions
providing for the recall of judges. No people, it seems to
me, are fit to come into the Union as States who are willing
to put the 'recall' of judges into their fundamental law.
Whether a particular Territory shall be admitted into the
Union as a State is a matter of discretion with Congress.
That discretion should be exercised so as to maintain sound
principles that are recognized as such by Anglo-Saxon people.
Upon the question whether the 'recall' of judges is republican in the constitutional sense, I express no opinion; for
that question may come up for judicial determination. I
only speak for the 'recall' as a matter of public policy."[4]

This is in itself an interesting doctrine. All recognize
certain things that a State may do which are not unconstitutional but which may not meet the approval of the other
States. Though a State may do these things after it is ad-

[4] Remarks of Blackburn Esterling, in ibid., p. 36.

mitted into the Union, it would not be wise for Congress to put itself on record as approving them by admitting new States with such provisions in their constitutions. It would be far better for the State to break its promise, so far as the nation is concerned, after it had been admitted into the Union, than it would be for Congress to sanction the obnoxious provisions.

As a hearer of arguments Justice Harlan was more than a scrutinizer of points made by lawyers; he sometimes sought to train the lawyer who argued before the court. The following story with regard to this trait is told by a lawyer: " Something like two years ago I was called here to argue a case in which a sovereign State was the complainant, and my associate was a talented young lawyer who was letter perfect in that case, but who had never before appeared in this court. The matter was to be presented on a motion for which under the rules as they stood, an hour was allowed on each side, and I suggested that my associate should open case, intending that if he presented it satisfactorily I would leave him to occupy the entire time alloted to us; but he was so full of his case that he began the presentation of it in a way that would have required hours. I was growing a little nervous over the situation myself, but I hesitated to interrupt him, because I thought it might confuse him, and just as I was debating with myself what it was best to do, Judge Harlan called on him in a stern voice to 'come to your point.' My young friend, confused beyond description, managed to say that he was coming to it; but Judge Harlan replied that his time would be consumed before he reached it, and that in the meantime the court would have no idea of the question he was presenting to it. It was a trying experience for a new member of the bar, and I felt it so keenly that I shared the young man's resentment. A few days afterwards I happened to meet Judge Harlan as he was coming to the Capitol, and told him bluntly that I regarded his rebuke of that young man as a little less than cruel. Instead of exhibiting an irritation, which would have been entirely permissible against a member of his bar who had presumed to criticise his conduct, he turned to me, and, smiling said: 'My dear Senator, you do not understand my purpose. I saw that the young man was embarrassed by his surroundings, and I desired to relieve him from embarrassment.' I told him that I thought he had chosen a curious way of producing such a result, and he advised me to watch that young man when he next appeared in this court. It so happened that a reargument of that very case was ordered, and when my associate and myself appeared here to argue it at the next term, I found Judge Harlan's remedy for a lawyer's embarrassment completely justified."[5]

Few adverse criticisms have been made of Mr. Harlan as a judge. He was a militant justice, but his militancy was on the side of law. Even with the many dissents rendered by him there is no evidence of hard feeling on the part of his associates. He did not bear malice with his disagreement, but he was often very vehement in his dissents.

His opinions and dissents often contained extraneous matter, that is, reference to circumstances which had no direct bearing upon the case. But these are easily passed over when one is looking for his argument. The presence of these digressions is more an evidence of his general interest in the public than it is of his lack of knowledge of the principles of legal argumentation.

Some have claimed that Justice Harlan emphasized too greatly the letter of the law. Such a contention is based either on ignorance or on prejudice. One illustration will show this point. No one who so interpreted the eleventh amendment as to maintain that a suit against the officer of a State in his official capacity was not a suit against a State could have held to the strict letter of the law. When, by a logical and grammatical construction a law could be made to correct the evils intended to be remedied by it, he argued that this should be done. But if such an application meant an absolute change in the law, he held that this change should be left to the legislative power. The criticism that he stressed too emphatically the letter of the law arises from the fact that he did not believe in equivocation.

---

[5] Remarks of Joseph W. Bailey, in ibid., pp. 21–22.

CHAPTER I

SUABILITY OF STATES

The suability or non-suability of a State has been before the Supreme Court of the United States in numerous instances. It has arisen under various circumstances, and the court has given on this question many opinions which it is difficult to reconcile. It is a complicated question, and no attempt will be made to give an exposition of the whole matter. Interest centers around Justice Harlan and the views which he has held on the subject. He had a very decided opinion on this point, and he almost never failed to assert himself whenever the matter was before the court.

Article i, section 10 of the constitution of the United States places the following prohibition upon the States: "No State shall . . . pass any . . . law impairing the obligation of contracts"; and the fourteenth amendment provides that "no State shall . . . deprive any person of life, liberty or property, without due process of law." But the eleventh amendment expressly stipulates that the courts of the United States may not entertain a suit against a State. Suppose, therefore, a State takes property without due process of law for its own use or passes a law impairing the obligation of its own contracts, what action can the individual take in order to receive the benefit of these stipulations? Such a question, of course, opens up the whole problem as to what is to be termed a suit against a State, for if the law takes property without due process of law or impairs the obligation of contracts, the law is unconstitutional even though the State itself be a party to the proceedings. At the same time, if the action to prevent the enforcement of the law amounts to a suit against the State, it cannot be maintained. Therefore, the problem is almost that of an irresistible force meeting an immovable body. Shall the immunity from compulsory judicial process be upheld, or shall the prohibitions relative to contracts and due process of law be enforced? In many cases one or the other but not both of these ends can be realized. It is clear that here there is abundant opportunity for difference of opinion according to which one of these constitutional mandates is maximized and which one minimized. As will be found, the court has sought to maintain a middle course, and in so doing has not always been consistent in the doctrines which it has declared.

Discussion of Cases.—Justice Harlan's views with reference to this subject appear especially in the dissents which he rendered in Louisiana v. Jumel, 107 U. S. 711, and Ex parte Young, 209 U. S. 123. The first, Louisiana v. Jumel, decided that a certain action against the treasurer of the State of Louisiana was a suit against the State and hence could not be entertained; while the other, Ex parte Young, decided that a certain action against the attorney-general of Minnesota did not constitute a suit against a State and hence could be entertained by the court. In neither of these cases was the action on account of any private act of the person concerned, but because of the official acts of each. The fact that the latter decision allowed the suit and the former did not makes the cases typical; and the fact that Justice Harlan dissented from each affords an opportunity to deduce from them his exact opinion on this subject.

The case of Louisiana v. Jumel was decided in 1882. The facts in the case were briefly these: The legislature of Louisiana provided in 1874 for an issue of bonds, for the purpose of consolidating and reducing the floating and bonded debt. The bonds were to be payable to the bearer forty years from January 1, 1874, and to bear interest at the rate of seven per cent, payable the first of January of each year. The bonds were to be signed by the governor, the auditor, and the secretary of state, and the coupons by the auditor and the treasurer. The State levied a tax for the purpose of meeting the above obligations, and immediately thereafter passed an amendment to the constitution making the bonds create a valid contract between the State and every holder of such bonds, which the State could in no wise impair. Certain persons held bonds to the amount of $20,000 and unpaid coupons, due January 1, 1880, to the amount of $79,900.

On the first day of January, 1880, a new constitution of Louisiana went into effect. A portion of that constitution aimed to alter the former provisions of 1874. It reduced the interest to be paid on the consolidated bonds from seven per cent to two, and further stipulated that coupons of said consolidated bonds falling due on the first day of January, 1880, should be remitted, and that the proceeds of the taxes which had been collected for the purpose of meeting these obligations, of which there were $300,000 in the treasury, should go to defray other expenses of the State.

Holders who presented their bonds for payment were refused because of this action of the State, whereupon they contended that this action of the State impaired the obligation of contracts. They therefore brought suit against the treasurer of the State to compel him to make payment according to the previous legislation of the State. The state treasurer entered the plea that such a suit was a suit against the State and as such was forbidden by the eleventh amendment to the Constitution of the United States. The circuit court of the United States pronounced this a valid plea, and upon appeal to the Supreme Court this decision was sustained.

The grounds for this decision were these: It was evident that the State designed to make promises and pledges in such a manner that they would be protected by the Constitution of the United States; and that the State, in adopting the debt ordinance of 1879, designed to stop further levy of the promised tax and to prevent the disbursing officer from using the revenue from previous levies to pay the interest falling due January 1, 1880, as well as the principal and interest maturing thereafter. If the State could be sued, there was little doubt that this later state action would be pronounced an impairment of the obligation of the State's contract. The question was whether the contract could be enforced, notwithstanding the provision in the new state constitution, by coercing the agents and officers of the State, whose authority to act had been withdrawn, without the State itself being made a party to the proceedings. By the original statute these officers were directed to use the money in the treasury in one way; by the new constitution they were directed to use it in another way; by the statute they had to raise more money by taxation, but by the constitution it was ordered that this should not be done. The officers owed their duty to the State, and had no contract relations with the bondholders. They could be moved through the State, but not the State through them. In short, then, the officers had always to obey the will of the State, and if this will changed the action of the officers had to change accordingly.

The first precedent cited by the Supreme Court was Reg. v. Lords Com. of the Treas., Law Rep. 7 Q. B. 387, in which the court of Queen's Bench of England refused to take cognizance of a case when an amount of money had been raised for a specific purpose and appropriated by Parliament for another purpose. In this case it was held that a suit entered against the Lords Commissioners of the Treasury was a suit against the sovereign and not valid. The Supreme Court of the United States claimed a similarity between the two cases in that the former was a suit against the commissioners of the treasury of England, and the latter was against the state treasurer of Louisiana.

As to this point, Justice Harlan in his dissent said: " It seems to me that case furnishes no support for the suggestion that these are suits against the State, simply because they are brought against its officers. It does not conflict with the proposition that the state Treasurer can be compelled to apply the proceeds of these taxes as stipulated in the Statute and Constitution of 1874, which were his sole authority to receive them. Here *is a statutable* obligation upon him to pay the coupons as they matured. And to that is added the obligation imposed by that Constitution, which, in terms, declares that the proceeds of taxes collected under the Act of that year ' Shall be paid by the Treasurer of the State to the holders of said bonds, as the principal and interest of the same shall fall due,' without further legislative authority. These obligations remain upon that officer, unless it be that the Debt Ordinance, although unconstitutional and void, has discharged them. Had Parliament, instead of the Act involved in the case cited, passed one directly imposing upon the defendants the duty of paying out of moneys appropriated for that purpose a certain class of claims, it is manifest that the court of Queen's Bench would have compelled them, by *mandamus* or other process, to perform that duty. In the case supposed, there would have been a statutable obligation which the court would not have permitted the defendants to evade on the pretext that they were officers of the Crown." Hereupon Justice Harlan cites a case in which this very condition arose and in which the court issued such a mandamus, and shows further that the fact that the Constitution of the United States forbids that any State impair the obligation of contracts makes more powerful the statutory force; and further that the difference in the nature of the sovereign in England from that of the sovereign here shows that little weight should be given to the English decision.

In short, then, Justice Harlan's reply was this: The English court did not entertain the suit because there was a statutable obligation upon them not to do so; the American courts should have entertained the suit because there was a statutable obligation upon them to do so,—a statutable obligation not altered because of the unconstitutional amendment which tried to relieve Louisiana of its duly contracted debts.

The next case cited by the court for precedent is Osborn v. Bank of the United States, 9 Wheat. 738. The argument of the majority opinion is that there was a great difference between this case and the Louisiana case. In the Osborn case "the object was to prevent money which had been unlawfully taken out of the bank by the officers of the State from getting into the Treasury. . . . Thus the money seized was kept out of the Treasury, because if it got in, it would be irretrievably lost to the bank, since the State could not be sued to recover it back. No one pretended that if the money had been actually paid into the Treasury, and had become mixed with the other money there, it could have been got back from the State by a suit against the officers. They would have been individually liable for the unlawful seizure and conversion, but the recovery would be against them individually for the wrongs they had personally done, and could have no effect on the money which was held by the State. Certainly no one would ever suppose that by a proceeding against the officers alone, they could be held as trustees for the bank, and required to set apart from the moneys in the Treasury an amount equal to that which had been improperly put there, and hold it for the discharge of the liability which the State incurred by reason of the unlawful exaction."

Justice Harlan in his comment on this reasoning said: "The latter was a suit to recover moneys, which officers of the State of Ohio, in conformity with its statutes, had illegally taken from a bank of the United States. The suit being against the officers of the State, the objection was taken that it could not be sustained without the State itself being a party; that the State could not be sued; consequently, it was argued, the relief prayed (the restoration of the money) could not be granted. But to that objection the court, speaking by *Chief Justice* Marshall, . . . said: 'If the State of Ohio could have been made a party defendant, it can scarcely be denied that this would be a strong case for an injunction. The objection is that, as the real party cannot be brought before the court; a suit cannot be sustained against the agents of that party; and cases have been cited to show that a court of chancery will not make a decree unless all those who are substantially interested be made parties to the suit. This is certainly true where it is in the power of the plaintiff to make them parties; but if the person who is the real principal, the person who is the true source of the mischief, by whose power and for whose advantage it is done, be himself above the law, be exempt from all judicial process, it would be subversive of the best established principles to say that the laws could not afford the same remedies against the agent employed in doing the wrong, which they would afford against him could his principal be joined in the suit.' "

Justice Harlan noted that this decision had never been questioned before: " It seems to establish, upon grounds which cannot well be shaken, that a suit against state officers, to prevent a threatened wrong to the injury of the citizen, is not necessarily a suit against the State within the meaning of the 11th Amendment of the Constitution." Thus it appears that the argument on the part of the court was purely technical—it was rather in words than in meaning—and was, as Justice Harlan makes clear, a departure from what the court had previously maintained.

Davis v. Gray, 16 Wall. 203, is next mentioned by the court as affording grounds for its decision: In a land grant the receiver of a railroad "obtained an injunction against the Governor and Commissioner of the Land-Office of Texas to restrain them from incumbering, by patents to others, lands which had been contracted to the railroad company. . . . The specific tracts of land in dispute were, by the contract which had been made, segregated from the public domain and set apart for the company. The case rests on the same principle it would if patents had been actually issued to the company, and the State, through its officers, was attempting to place a cloud on the title by granting subsequent patents to others."

Justice Harlan recognized that a full statement of the

point at issue is sufficient to make the citation argue against the conclusion of the court. He says: "In that case it appears that the State of Texas made a grant of lands to a railroad company, upon the basis of which bonds were issued known as land-grant mortgage bonds. They were sold in large numbers in this country and Europe. Subsequently the State, by provisions of its statutes and Constitution, attempted to repudiate and nullify its contract; and, in pursuance thereof, its officers proposed to issue patents to others for a part of the lands embraced in this grant. Thereupon a suit in equity was instituted in the Circuit Court of the United States against the Governor and the Commissioner of the General Land-Office of Texas, to prevent them from issuing patents for the lands or any part of them. The State was, of course, not made a party on the record. The bill was demurred to upon the ground that she could not be sued, and that the suit, being against her officers, was one, within the meaning of the Constitution, against her. The demurrer was overruled, and the relief asked was given."

He further explained that Justice Swayne, in rendering this decision, stated the following principles as having been announced in Osborn v. Bank of the United States: "1. A Circuit Court of the United States, in a proper case in equity, may enjoin a state officer from executing a state law in conflict with the Constitution, or a statute of the United States, when such execution will violate the rights of the complainant. 2. Where the State is concerned, the State should be made a party, if it can be done. That it cannot be done, is a sufficient reason for the omission to do it, and the court may proceed to decree against the officers of the State in all respects as if the State were a party to the record. 3. In deciding who are parties to the suit, the court will not look beyond the record. Making a state officer a party does not make the State a party, although her laws prompt his action and the State stands behind him as the real party in interest. . . . It was in conformity with those doctrines that the relief asked was given."

Two other cases were referred to in the argument for the court, namely, Board of Liquidation v. McComb, 92 U. S. 531, which arose under the same act as the case now under consideration, and United States v. Lee, 106 U. S. 196. It is hardly necessary to discuss these cases further, for the same sort of distinction was made by the court, and equally conclusive replies were made by Justice Harlan. Both were suits entertained against officers, the former against an officer of Louisiana, and the latter against officers of the United States. In both the officers were sued in their official capacity and the decisions were rendered against them.

In closing his dissent, Justice Harlan said: " My own conclusions are: That the officers of Louisiana cannot rightfully execute provisions of its constitution which conflict with the supreme law of the land, and the courts of the Union should not permit them to do so;

" That but for the adoption of the unconstitutional Debt Ordinance of 1879, and whether the suits were in a state court or in the Circuit Court of the United States, these state officers would have been restrained by injunction from diverting the funds collected to meet the interest on the consolidated bonds, and would have been compelled, by *mandamus*, to perform the purely ministerial duties enjoined by the Statute and Constitution of 1874;

" That if, by existing laws, the Circuit Court of the United States has no power to issue such writs, still, upon the removal of the *mandamus* suit from the state court, the former had power to do what the state court could legally have done had there been no removal; *viz.:* make peremptory the alternative *mandamus* granted at the beginning of the suit by the inferior state court;

" That the Debt Ordinance being void because in conflict with the Constitution of the United States, furnishes no reason whatever, least of all in the courts of the Union, why the relief asked should not be granted by any court of proper jurisdiction as to parties;

"That to refuse relief because of the command of a State to its officer to do that which is forbidden, and refrain from doing that which is enjoined, by the supreme law of the land; or to give effect, for any purpose, in the courts of the Union, to the orders of the supreme political power of a State, made in defiance of the Constitution of the United States, is, practically, to announce that, so far as judicial action is concerned, a State may, by nullifying provisions in its fundamental law, destroy rights of contract, the obligation of which the Constitution declares shall not be impaired by any state law. To such a doctrine, I can never give my assent."

In Ex parte Young, 209 U. S. 123, there appears to be the same sort of contention as that which arose in Louisiana v. Jumel. In this case, however, the court decided that an injunction against the attorney-general of the State of Minnesota issued by the circuit court of the United States to prevent his putting into effect certain laws would hold, in spite of the plea that such an action was against the State of Minnesota.

The case arose after a number of decisions along the same line as Louisiana v. Jumel, in all of which Justice Harlan consistently asserted the doctrine which he had just announced. A statement at the beginning of his dissent in the Young case might seem to indicate that he had given up the theory which he had so tenaciously held, but as his argument is examined more deeply this is found not to be true. His doctrine is essentially the same, and this case had made him alter only slightly one phase of it. This point will be explained later. The words are as follows: "Although the history of this litigation is set forth in the opinion of the court, I deem it appropriate to restate the principal facts of the case in direct connection with my examination of the question upon which the decision turns. . . . That examination, I may say at the outset, is entered upon with no little embarrassment, in view of the fact that the views expressed by me are not shared by my brethren.

I may also frankly admit embarrassment arising from certain views stated in dissenting opinions heretofore delivered by me which did not, at the time, meet the approval of my brethren, and which I do not now myself entertain. What I shall say in this opinion will be in substantial accord with what the court has heretofore decided, while the opinion of the court departs, as I think, from principles previously announced by it upon full consideration. I propose to adhere to former decisions of the court, whatever may have been once my opinion as to certain aspects of this general question."

When his arguments are examined more closely it is found that the "certain views stated in dissenting opinions heretofore delivered by me . . . which I do not now myself entertain" refer only incidentally to his general doctrine as to the suability of a State, for, as will be seen, his real opinion on this question comes out more clearly in this dissent than in any of the others.

Upon examination, the case of Ex parte Young is found to be a very difficult one. It was an action brought in the circuit court of the United States by a railroad company to prevent the State of Minnesota from enforcing certain laws which the company claimed were confiscatory and hence deprived them of property without due process of law. The acts were so stringent in their nature as to make it almost impossible for the company to have their case tried in any court to test the validity thereof. For this reason the complainants alleged that the above-mentioned orders and acts deprived them of the equal protection of the laws, and also deprived them of their property without due process of law, and hence were unconstitutional and void. The acts were very stringent because of the following characteristics: In the first place, it was practically impossible to have their constitutionality tested because of the severe penalties imposed if the Supreme Court should pronounce them constitutional. They could get no officer or employee of the railroad company to take the risk. In the second place, the fines for breaking the laws were so great as almost to put the company out of business before the Supreme Court could pass on it. About the only recourse that the railroad had was to get the United States circuit court to issue an injunction forbidding the state attorney-general to put these laws into operation. This was done; and the Supreme Court sustained the writ.

With the issue clearly understood, the nature of the arguments of the court and of Justice Harlan's dissent can be examined. The question, of course, for the court to decide was whether such an injunction constituted a suit against the State within the meaning of the eleventh amendment to the Constitution, as was contended by the attorney-general of the State.

Justice Peckham, speaking for the court, in his preliminary remarks said: "We have, therefore, upon this record, the case of an unconstitutional act of the state legislature and an intention by the attorney-general of the state to endeavor to enforce its provisions, to the injury of the company, in compelling it, at great expense, to defend legal proceedings of a complicated and unusual character, and involving questions of vast importance to all employees and officers of the company, as well as to the company itself. The question that arises is whether there is a remedy that the parties interested may resort to, by going into a Federal court of equity, in a case involving a violation of the Federal Constitution, and obtaining a judicial investigation of the problem, and, pending its solution, obtain freedom from suits, civil or criminal, by a temporary injunction, and, if the question be finally decided favorably to the contention of the company, a permanent injunction restraining all such actions or proceedings." Many cases are cited which have involved the question of the suability of States, but the line of sequence attempted to be established by these citations is difficult to follow.

Justice Harlan said: "If a suit be commenced in a state court, and involves a right secured by the Federal Constitution, the way is open under our incomparable judicial system to protect that right, first, by the judgment of the state court, and ultimately by the judgment of this court, upon writ of error. But such right cannot be protected by means of a suit which, at the outset, is directly or in legal effect, one against the state whose action is alleged to be illegal. That mode of redress is absolutely forbidden by the 11th Amendment, and cannot be made legal by mere construction, or by any consideration of the consequences that may follow from the operation of the statute. Parties cannot, in any case, obtain redress by a suit *against the state*. Such has been the uniform ruling in this court, and it is most unfortunate that it is now declared to be competent for a Federal circuit court, by exerting its authority over the chief law officer of the state, without the consent of the state, to exclude the state, in its sovereign capacity, from its own courts when seeking to have the ruling of those courts as to its powers under its own statutes. Surely, the right of a state to invoke the jurisdiction of its own courts is not less than the right of individuals to invoke the jurisdiction of a Federal court. The preservation of the dignity and sovereignty of the states, within the limits of their constitutional powers, is of the last importance, and vital to the preservation of our system of government. The courts should not permit themselves to be driven by the hardships, real or supposed, of particular cases, to accomplish results, even if they be just results, in a mode forbidden by the fundamental law."

Referring to In re Ayers, 123 U. S. 443, a case in which a suit against the attorney-general of the State of Virginia had been pronounced a suit against the State and hence void, Justice Harlan, apparently to show how far the present decision was inconsistent with others, made the following remarks: "The proceeding against the attorney-general of Virginia had for its object to compel, by indirection, the performance of the contract which that commonwealth was alleged to have made with bondholders,—such performance, on the part of the State, to be effected by means of orders in a Federal circuit court directly controlling the official action of that officer. The proceedings in the . . . suit against the attorney-general of Minnesota had for its object, by means of orders in a Federal circuit court, directed to that officer, *to control the action of that state* in reference to the enforcement of certain statutes by judicial proceedings commenced in its own courts. The relief sought in each case was to control the state *by controlling the conduct of its law officer, against its will.* I cannot conceive how the proceeding against the attorney-general of Virginia could be deemed a suit against that state, and yet the proceeding against the attorney-general of Minnesota is not to be deemed a suit against Minnesota, when the object and effect of the latter proceeding was, beyond all question, to shut that state entirely out of its own courts, and prevent it, through its law officer, from invoking their jurisdiction in a special matter of public concern, involving official duty, about which the state desired to know the views of its own judiciary. In my opinion the decision in the Ayers case determines this case for the petitioners." As Justice Harlan had dissented from the Ayers case, it would appear from the above that he is pleading with the court at least to stand by something.

Since the concern in this case is not so much with Justice Harlan's replies to arguments given by the court as with his opinion definitely stated, it will be well to note his quotation from Fitts v. McGhee, 172 U. S. 516, in which case he had written the opinion: "'In support of the contention that the present suit is not one against the state, reference was made by counsel to several cases. . . . Upon examination it will be found that the defendants in each of those cases were officers of the state, specially charged with the execution of a state enactment alleged to be unconstitutional, but under the authority of which, it was averred, they were committing or were about to commit some specific wrong or trespass to the injury of the plaintiff's rights. There is a wide difference between a suit against individuals holding official positions under a state, to prevent them, under the sanction of an unconstitutional statute, from committing by some positive act a wrong or trespass, and a suit against officers of a state merely to test the constitutionality of a state statute, in the enforcement of which those officers will act only by formal judicial proceedings in the courts of the state. In the present case, as we have said, neither of the state officers named held any special relation to the particular statute alleged to be unconstitutional. They were not expressly directed to see to its enforcement. If, because they were law officers of the state, a case could be made for the purpose of testing the constitutionality of the statute by an injunction suit brought against them, then the constitutionality of every act passed by the legislature could be tested by a suit against the governor and the attorney-general, based upon the theory that the former as the executive of the state was, in a general sense, charged with the execution of all its laws, and the latter, as attorney-general, might represent the state in litigation involving the enforcement of its statutes. That would be a very convenient way for obtaining a speedy judicial determination of questions of constitutional law which may be raised by individuals, but it is a mode which cannot be applied to the states of the Union consistently with the fundamental principle that they cannot, without their assent, be brought into any court at the suit of private persons. If their officers commit acts of trespass or wrong to the citizen, they may be individually proceeded against for such trespasses or wrong. Under the view we take of the question, the citizen is not without effective remedy, when proceeded against under a legislative enactment void for repugnancy to the supreme law of the land; for, whatever the form of proceeding against him, he can make his defense upon the ground that the statute is unconstitutional and void. And that question can be ultimately brought to this court for final determination.' . . . The Fitts case is not overruled, but is, I fear, frittered away or put out of sight by unwarranted distinctions."

The fact that Justice Harlan in this dissent quoted approvingly from Fitts v. McGhee the opinion as to what should be regarded as the law relating to suits against state officers shows that his embarrassment at the change of view which he had undergone did not mean that he had entirely given up his theory. It rather indicates that he had formed more clearly within his own mind exactly what was his doctrine. The case of Ex parte Young had brought one phase of the subject before him which apparently he had not fully appreciated till then, that is, the possibility that a citizen, by means of an injunction issued by a circuit court of the United States, could stay the action of the State in the enforcement of its laws. To that extent, then, he seems to have changed his mind, but no further. The above quotation puts as clearly as can be put Justice Harlan's opinion of the extent to which the interpretation of the eleventh amendment should go. In brief, it might be stated as follows: Everything that might arise in a judicial way that would involve an officer in his public capacity ought not to be deemed a suit against the State, and hence invalid. And if an officer of the State should be called into court because of a definite act on his part, so long as the averment was made that he was acting under an unconstitutional statute he should be made to answer. His objection to the decision in Ex parte Young seems to be twofold, however. The first objection was that the officer was proceeded against under an averment that the general provisions of the statute were unconstitutional rather than for a definite act on his part under a statute the constitutionality of which was challenged. In the second place, he objected because by such action the circuit court was blocking the legal processes of the State. Through this means the court had given to the individual the power to halt the action of the State, and had therefore in essence violated the Constitution of the United States in abridging the powers duly allowed to the States by that instrument.

These two cases show clearly Justice Harlan's opinion as to what should be the interpretation of the phrase " suits

against States." It remains, however, to be seen, by means
of a brief comment on other dissents and opinions rendered
by him on this subject, how consistently he held to this
principle.

The decision of Louisiana v. Jumel was given in 1882.
At that time Justice Harlan had been on the bench only five
years. This case marks the first departure of the court
from what seemed to be a well-established precedent as to
the meaning of the eleventh amendment. Usually Justice
Harlan was not very careful to avoid extraneous matter in
his dissents, but in this case it was not so. Probably no
other of his dissents surpasses this one in clear and concise
reasoning. From this point on to the case of Ex parte
Young will be traced his opinions and dissents in the more
important cases which have included that question. The
most important cases are: Antoni v. Greenhow, 107 U. S.
769; Cunningham v. Macon and Brunswick R. Co., 109 U.
S. 446; Hapgood v. Southern, 117 U. S. 52; In re Ayers,
123 U. S. 443; Belknap v. Schild, 161 U. S. 10; Fitts v.
McGhee, 172 U. S. 516; Tindal v. Wesley, 167 U. S. 204;
International Postal Supply Co. v. Bruce, 194 U. S. 601.

In the case of Antoni v. Greenhow the vexed question of
the suability of States came up only incidentally. This
case was decided next after Louisiana v. Jumel, and involved a similar situation. In 1871 Virginia passed a law
making the interest coupons of a bond issue receivable at
and after maturity for all taxes, debts, dues, and demands
of the State. Later the General Assembly passed another
act prohibiting the officers in charge of the collection of
taxes from receiving in payment anything else than gold,
coin, and so on. Subsequent to the passage of this act making it unlawful to accept such coupons for taxes one An-
drew Antoni attempted to pay taxes with interest coupons.
Upon the refusal of the officer to accept them, Antoni took
the matter into court. The question was taken to the Supreme Court of the United States by writ of error on the
ground that this subsequent legislation was an impairment

of the obligation of contracts. By nice distinctions it was decided that such action on the part of the State did not impair the obligation of contracts, and the question of suability was put aside as not being of necessity decided in this case.

Justice Harlan, still warm from his dissent in the Louisiana case, made the following remark: " It should be remembered that the court places its decision upon the ground that the change in the remedy has not, in legal effect, impaired the obligation of the contract, and not upon the ground that this suit is, within the meaning of the Federal Constitution, a suit against the State. Nor could it be placed upon the latter ground without overturning the settled doctrines of this court. . . . It is a case in which a plain official duty, requiring no exercise of discretion, is to be performed, and where performance in the mode stipulated by the contract is refused."

Cunningham v. Macon and Brunswick R. Co. brings up again the interpretation of the eleventh amendment. The facts in this case were as follows: The State of Georgia endorsed the bonds of a railroad company, taking a lien upon the railroad as security. The company failing to pay interest upon endorsed bonds, the governor of the State took possession of the road, and put it into the hands of a receiver, who made sale of it to the State. The State took possession of it, and took up the endorsed bonds, substituting the bonds of the State in their place. The holders of the mortgage bonds issued by the railroad company subsequently to those endorsed by the State, but before the default in payment of interest, filed a bill in equity to foreclose their own mortgage and set aside the said sale and to be let in as a prior in lien, for other relief affecting the property, and set forth the above facts and made the governor and the treasurer of the State parties. Those officers demurred, and it was held that the State was so much interested in the property that relief could not be granted without making it a party, and that the court was without jurisdiction.

The argument of the court was very similar to that in Louisiana v. Jumel. Without going into the content of Justice Harlan's dissent, his opinion may be summarized as follows: In deciding the case the court had overlooked certain vital points which would have proved that the State was not legally in possession of the property. Hence the suit against the officers of the State should have been entertained to establish this fact, and to put the property into the hands of the legal owners. The court in this case seemed to say that the mere plea of possession in the name of the State exempts from suit, whereas Justice Harlan desired that the legal status of this possession be established and that this be done by entertaining a suit against the officers of the State.

In Hapgood v. Southern, another case involving the issue of bonds, the same question was to be answered as in Louisiana v. Jumel. Justice Harlan admitted that this case was governed by that decision, but denied again the rightfulness of it.

Since the case of In re Ayers has been referred to and sufficiently explained, it is unnecessary to go further into its details. In his dissent from this case Justice Harlan quoted approvingly a precedent cited in United States v. Lee from Osborn v. Bank of United States as follows: "Where the State is concerned, the State should be made a party, if it can be done. That it cannot be done is a sufficient reason for the omission to do it, and the court may proceed to decree against the officers of the State in all respects as if the State were a party to the record. In deciding who are parties to the suit, the court will not look beyond the record. Making a state officer a party does not make the State a party, *although her law may have prompted his action, and the State may stand behind him as a real party in interest.* A State can be made a party only by shaping the bill expressly with that view, as where individuals or corporations are intended to be put in that relation to the case."

In the following quotation from Justice Harlan's dissent

from Belknap v. Schild is found a good illustration of his vehemence when he opposed vigorously the decision of the court: "If the United States may appropriate to public use the invention of a patentee, without his consent, and without liability to suit, as upon implied contract, for the value of the use of such invention; if, as the court holds, a public officer acting only in the interest of the public is not individually liable for gains, profits, and advantages that may accrue to the United States from such use; and if the officer who thus violates the rights of the patentee cannot be restrained by injunction,—then the government may well be regarded as organized robbery so far as the rights of patentees are concerned."

It had been decided by the court that in a suit in equity brought by the patentee of an improvement in caisson gates against officers of the United States, who were using in their official capacity at a dry dock in a navy yard a caisson gate made and used by the United States in infringement of his patent, the plaintiff is not entitled to an injunction. Nor can he recover profits if the only profit proved is a saving to the United States in the cost of the gate.

The case of Fitts v. McGhee, in which the decision was rendered by Justice Harlan himself, gave an excellent opportunity for him to express by way of dictum what he seemed so much to desire should become law. The question was the validity of a statute of Alabama which established a maximum rate of tolls for a bridge across the Tennessee River. The owners of the bridge claimed that since this rate did not allow them reasonable compensation it took their property without due process of law. The United States circuit court took cognizance of the case, held that the act was unconstitutional, and issued an injunction against the officers of the State to prevent them from arresting the bridge officials. It was taken to the Supreme Court on the plea that such an injunction was à suit against the State within the meaning of the eleventh amendment.

The decision was rendered, however, on the jurisdiction of the circuit court. Its decision was reversed on the ground that it had taken jurisdiction over something which should have been settled in the state courts and appealed, if necessary, by writ of error to the United States Supreme Court. In this case, however, is found the first clear statement of Justice Harlan's real opinion as to what should be the law regarding suits against officers of a State. It was quoted in his dissent from Ex parte Young and noted above, namely, that suits against officers, though for acts done in their official capacity, should be entertained if a definite damage had been averred under the statute supposed to be unconstitutional.

In Tindal v. Wesley Justice Harlan was also called upon to deliver the opinion of the court. This case was to test the legality of the title to certain land held in South Carolina in the name of the State. The defendants, officers of the State, seem to have got possession of it by paying for it with a kind of paper issue which was practically worthless. The possession of the land by the State of South Carolina corresponded very significantly to the possession of the Lee estate by the United States, in that the rightful owners had not been duly paid for their property. In this case Justice Harlan extended to the States the principle set forth in the Lee case. He referred largely to the latter decision. In the case of Tindal v. Wesley is seen a comparatively recent decision in which a suit against officers of a State in their official capacity was entertained and decided against them.

The next and last case in this connection is that of the International Postal Supply Co. v. Bruce. The decision in this case was brief and concise, but the dissent was lengthy. Justice Holmes rendered the decision. Justice Harlan dissented. His dissent held the same contention, but it showed some new features. He said at the outset: " The United States is not here sued, although, as in *United States* v. *Lee,* it may be incidentally affected by the result. No decree is asked against it. The suit is against Dwight H. Bruce, who is proceeding in violation of the plaintiff's right of property, and denies the power of any court to interfere with him, solely upon the ground that what he is doing is under the order and sanction of the Postoffice Department. He is, so to speak, in the possession of, and wrongfully using, the plaintiff's patented invention, and denies the right of any court, by its mandatory order, to prevent him from continuing in his lawless invasion of a right granted by the Constitution and laws of the United States."

This suit was brought against the postmaster by the owner of letters patent on a machine for canceling and postmarking. Its purpose was to restrain this postmaster from using such infringing machines, which had been hired from the manufacturer by the Postoffice Department for a term not yet expired. The gist of the argument for the court appears in the following sentences: "In the case at bar the United States is not the owner of the machines, it is true, but it is a lessee in possession, for a term which has not expired. It has a property,—a right *in rem*,—in the machines, which, though less extensive than absolute ownership, has the same incident of a right to use them while it lasts. This right cannot be interfered with behind its back; and, as it cannot be made a party, this suit, like that of *Belknap* v. *Schild,* must fail. The answer to the question certified must be ' No.' Whether or not a renewal of the lease could be enjoined is not before us."

It appears, then, that it was not the fact that the decision was against the patentee which aroused Justice Harlan's ire, but it was the precedent which the peculiar wording of the decision seemed to set. He could not justify in his mind the infringement on the part of the United States of a patentee's rights. It was this precedent which he was citing when he said: " I am of opinion that every officer of the government, however high his position, may be prevented by injunction, operating directly upon him, from illegally injuring or destroying the property rights of the citizen; and this relief should more readily be given when the government itself cannot be made a party of record." Yet the decision seems to hold that the government may use patented articles regardless of the rights of the patentee, because of the fact that there is no way to stay the action of the government by enjoining the officer. It must be added that by an act of 1910 Congress has provided that such persons may appeal to the court of claims and get compensation. But this provision, of course, does not give full relief because it is necessary that a large amount of money be involved in order to get a case into that court. Nevertheless the government, if not the court, has to that extent come to accept Justice Harlan's doctrine.

Justice Harlan's Doctrine of Suability.—There seem to be mainly three grounds upon which an attempt is made to justify the theory of non-suability. The strongest has been aptly stated by Justice Miller in United States v. Lee: "It seems most probable that it has been adopted in our courts as a part of the general doctrine of publicists that the supreme power in every state, wherever it may reside, shall not be compelled, by process of courts of its own creation, to defend itself in those courts." This principle is given the most prominent place in a discussion of the development of the theory of non-suability of States in the United States.[1]

But it seems that this contention may be open to some objections, at least from Justice Harlan's standpoint. In fact, it may even be questioned whether this contention in essence conflicts with his theory of suability. To answer that necessitates a clear analysis of the meaning of terms. What is meant when it is said that the courts are the creation of the supreme power? What is meant by the supreme power? These questions, of course, have been discussed fully by students of political science generally. The con-

[1] K. Singewald, "The Doctrine of Non-suability of the State in the United States," in Johns Hopkins Studies, series xxviii, no. 3, p. 10.

sensus of opinion seems to be that this supreme power is the will of the people. This will is usually expressed in a convention which forms a constitution, and this constitution gives the courts their jurisdiction, or at least outlines the position which they are to occupy in the government. Does, then, a suit against an officer in his official capacity necessarily imply the bringing of this supreme power before a court for trial? The supreme power is the constitution. This constitution allows the legislature to make laws along certain lines. It also allows the courts to interpret these laws and to determine whether the laws made are along the line of the constitution. Why, then, should not the court, which is duly designated as the final arbiter of the constitutionality of laws, summon officers of the State and cause them to show that any law that involves the functionaries of the State is in accordance with the constitution? Why should it not make them justify their actions? Why should it·be considered legal for the State to allow its officers to act in a way as regards itself and the citizens of the State that would be pronounced wrong as regards the citizens in their relations to each other? How are we going to know that such an act is in accordance with the will of the State unless it can be proved? In other words, how can we say that such an action is in reality an expression of the will of that supreme power until all of the organs of the supreme power, designated by it to have a say in the matter, have either tacitly or expressly given their assent?

The second contention was voiced by Justice Gray in Briggs v. Light-Boat, 11 Allen 157, as follows: "The broader reason is that it would be inconsistent with the very idea of supreme executive power, and would endanger the performance of the public duties of the sovereign, to subject him to repeated suits as a matter of right, at the will of any citizen, and to submit to the judicial tribunals the control and disposition of his public property, his instruments and means of carrying on his government in war and in peace, and the money in his treasury."[2]

This assertion means that shutting out a whole class of cases would necessarily reduce the number of suits to be tried. But it also means a little more than that. It means that there would be shut out a particularly disturbing class, one that might make the government falter in the performance of its duties. But is this assumption valid? The answer must be that it is not. As the cases discussed have shown, the court has not succeeded sufficiently well in defining that class of cases to shut it out. As a matter of fact, it has aggravated the situation by allowing certain suits against officers in their official capacity, while refusing relief to others with an equally good claim to be heard. This uncertainty in the law has tended to increase the number of unconstitutional statutes passed. With this increase and with the uncertainty of the law has come the tendency to bring additional suits, and the situation has been made worse. If it were recognized once for all that officers may be sued, this tendency toward the passage of unconstitutional legislation would naturally be checked, and thus the number of suits testing this legislation would tend to lessen.

An additional very logical objection is made by Justice Holmes in Kawananakoa v. Polyblank, 205 U. S. 349: "A sovereign is exempt from suit, not because of any formal conception or obsolete theory, but on the logical and practical ground that there can be no legal right as against the authority that makes the law on which the right depends."

This objection sounds convincing, but a careful examination may reveal faulty premises. There is little reason why there could not be legal action against officers of States. In fact, it is practiced to no small extent on the continent of Europe. The one thing for which our nation stands is the submission of everybody to law. Why then should it be legal for officers of the government to commit acts in behalf of the state which are recognized as wrong for

---

[2] Singewald, p. 10.

individuals? Does not the fact that the supreme power has said that certain things are wrong between man and man imply that those things are wrong between the government and the citizens?

Moreover, concerning the ability of the court to enforce its decree upon the officers in question, it is only necessary to say that decrees seldom need to be enforced by compulsion,—except those of a criminal nature, and these are not in question here. A case would hardly rise which would require violence in enforcement, involving the interpretation of the Constitution. But even if it did, it is certain that no court would be foolish enough to entertain a suit against an officer whose consent was needed to enforce its decree. There will usually be a way around this, and there is no reason why the court should not go as far as it can in this regard, instead of pronouncing, at every little pretense, that an action against an officer is a suit against the State. Such an interpretation would almost certainly center public opinion more strongly upon the Constitution, and would tend to purify the fundamental law. The case of United States v. Lee seems to be a wise decision and to establish a worthy precedent.

A further objection might also be urged, namely, that such a doctrine as that for which Justice Harlan stood might intimidate officers. If this doctrine were recognized as constitutional, they might hesitate to enforce the laws for fear that the laws might be declared unconstitutional. This objection could hardly hold, for two reasons: In the first place, the officers would certainly not be individually responsible for acts done at the direction of the State. Since, then, their personal responsibility would be no greater, their refusal to obey would be useless. In the second place, the court can by mandamus force an officer to perform ministerial functions.

Viewing the subject in the light of the above reasons, there appear to be no grounds for real objection to Justice

Harlan's contention that a suit against an officer to prevent him from enforcing against an individual a definite provision of a law should be maintained in all cases in order to test the constitutionality of the law under which the action is taken. As a result of such an interpretation of the eleventh amendment the number of cases which would arise on account of the uncertainty of the law would almost certainly be lessened, as there would be less danger that a State would try to cover unconstitutional legislation under the plea of the non-suability of States. There is little reason why a State should allow its officers to commit acts which are considered wrong for its citizens to commit.

CHAPTER II

IMPAIRMENT OF THE OBLIGATION OF CONTRACTS

Since the question of the suability of States is so closely related to that of the obligation of contracts, it is natural that this subject should be considered next. Some of this discussion will be derived from cases which have been alluded to in the previous chapter, but whereas in that chapter the concern was with the suability phase, it is now with the contract phase.

The Constitution of the United States has two clauses which might prohibit a State from impairing the obligation of contracts. The first is the express provision, in article i, section 10, that no State shall pass any "law impairing the obligation of contracts"; the second provision is that portion of the fourteenth amendment which reads that no State shall deprive "any person of life, liberty or property, without due process of law." Either of these stipulations might have the meaning desired, but since there is the express prohibition in the original draft of the Constitution, the second has, of course, no great importance here.

The Relation of a State to its Contracts.—This question has already been somewhat discussed in the consideration of the suability of States. It will now be developed more fully.

The Supreme Court has decided that the acts of the States during the Civil War should, for the most part, be valid, except in so far as they were directly in aid of the rebellion. Whereas the court has tried to make this ruling as extensive as possible, Justice Harlan has, at times, stood for a somewhat narrower doctrine. The case of Keith v. Clark, 97 U. S. 454, illustrates this point. Here the court decided that notes issued by the Bank of Tennessee in the

43

year 1861, after the outbreak of the Civil War, should be received in payment of taxes. The facts of the case were these: In 1838 the State had stipulated in the charter of the bank that the notes of the bank should be received in payment of taxes. Subsequent to the war a man tendered forty dollars of these notes, issued during the war while the State was a member of the Confederacy. The question, therefore, was, did the refusal of the tax-collector, on authority of a state act, to accept the notes of the Bank of Tennessee issued while the State was in rebellion constitute an impairment of the obligation of contracts; or, better, was the act which authorized that refusal an impairment of the obligation of contracts, since the State had, when the bank was chartered, agreed to accept its notes for taxes? The court said that such a statute did not impair the obligation of contracts, and that the notes should have been accepted for taxes.

The reasons for the holding of the court were three: First, the State of Tennessee had never legally been out of the Union, and hence its acts during the war had to be reckoned with. Second, in spite of the fact that the States had so far succeeded in separating themselves from the Union as to establish usurping governments, yet even those governments could not be entirely overlooked; their acts should be accepted as far as could be done. A contrary doctrine, it was claimed, would be opposed to the powers inherent in every organized society. Third, since the record did not show that the notes had been issued in aid of rebellion, they ought to be considered as not having been issued for that purpose.

The ground upon which Justice Harlan rested his dissent was that the duly recognized State was not legally bound to accept acts which had been passed under usurping authority. Since the notes issued at this time were of little value, there was no reason for declaring the particular act invalid which forbade the acceptance of the notes. "They were," he said, "the obligations of an institution controlled and managed by a revolutionary usurping State Government, in its name, for its benefit, and to prevent the restoration of the lawful government. It was the revolutionary government which undertook to withdraw the State of Tennessee from its allegiance to the Federal Government and make it one of the Confederate States. When, therefore, the people of Tennessee, who recognized the authority of the United States, assembled in delegate convention, in January, 1865, it was quite natural and, in my judgment, not in violation of the Federal Constitution" for them to declare invalid bonds, notes, and so on, issued under the usurping government.

"There is some difficulty in defining precisely what Acts of the usurping State Government the restored State Government should have recognized as valid and binding. It may be true that there were some of them which should, upon grounds of public policy, have been recognized by the lawful government as valid and binding. It may be that the courts, in absence of any declaration to the contrary by the lawful government, should recognize certain Acts of the revolutionary government as *prima facie* valid. But I am unwilling to give my assent to the doctrine that the Constitution of the United States imposed upon the lawful Government of Tennessee an obligation, which this court must enforce, to cripple its own revenue, by receiving for its taxes bank-notes issued and used, under the authority of the usurping government, for the double purpose of maintaining itself and defeating the restoration of the lawful government in its proper relations in the Union."

Hence, though Justice Harlan would have recognized certain of the acts of the revolutionary governments as valid, he would have drawn a much stricter line than did the court. Above all, he would not have recognized the validity of acts which the reinstated government had attempted to make invalid, at least to such an extent as to make the government take depreciated money for taxes, for this in itself would have meant that the usurping government, even after the war, was working toward the weakening of the recognized legal government. He would have been less liberal in this regard, and would not have counteracted legislation which enabled the State to obtain valid money for its taxes, when there was sufficient reason for declaring constitutional the act which imposed this requirement.

Though the courts have been careful not to uphold laws impairing the obligation of contracts among individuals, they have not been so particular to see that a State should not impair its own contracts. As has been seen, they have usually succeeded in getting out of this situation by asserting the suits to be against the States. As was brought out in the first chapter, the case of Louisiana v. Jumel, 107 U. S. 711, well illustrated this point. Here no one questioned the fact that an amendment to the state constitution had impaired the obligation of contracts. The only question was whether any remedy at law could be found whereby this impairment could be thwarted. The court decided that since a suit could not be entertained against officers of a State in their official capacity, there was no remedy. As was pointed out, however, the courts have been irresolute in holding to this doctrine, while Justice Harlan was very resolute in opposing it. According to him, the contract of a State was even more sacred than that of a person, and the plea that the suit was against the State should not permit a State to violate the contract clause. As he argued in his dissent from Louisiana v. Jumel, he has argued even more vigorously in other cases.

The case of Antoni v. Greenhow, 107 U. S. 769, illustrates this, and is typical of the success of a State in repudiating its debt through indirect methods. In 1871 Virginia passed a law providing for a bond issue in order to float her public debt. In this act it was provided, among other things, that the interest coupons of the bonds should be receivable for taxes, and that if the collector should refuse to accept them in payment of taxes he could be forced by mandamus to do so.   In 1882 an act was passed which purported to counter-act an accumulation of fraudulent coupons.   It provided that no coupons should be accepted for taxes, and that all taxes must be paid in currency.   If anyone, however, should tender interest coupons, they could be received and the question as to their genuineness be submitted to a jury.   If they were held to be genuine, the money paid would be refunded. The question, then, was whether this act of 1882 impaired the obligation of contracts, and whether it was therefore unconstitutional.   The court said no.   So long as the coupons were still receivable for taxes the obligation was not impaired, and the method of receiving them was imma-terial.   In short, the change in remedy for non-acceptance from mandamus to jury trial did not mean an impairment of the obligation of contracts.

This decision did not meet with the approval of Justice Harlan.   He contended that a change in remedy which im-posed new and burdensome conditions upon the coupon holders to such an extent as to make the coupons in fact valueless in their hands was necessarily an impairment of the obligation which they evidenced.   The former act had made the coupons receivable for taxes, and had arranged for their acceptance to be enforced; the second act had granted that the coupons were receivable, but had made it impossible for the holders to have them accepted without going to greater expense than the value of the coupons.

In answer to the argument that counterfeit coupons might be presented, he said that if the collector did not know cer-tain coupons to be valid there were sufficient means of veri-fication.   All that the tax collector had to do was to refuse them, and when the holder applied for a mandamus to force their acceptance there was opportunity to have the coupons tested.   The act of 1882, therefore, was neither expedient nor constitutional, and could not obtain his assent.

Following upon Antoni v. Greenhow was the case of Ex parte Ayers, 123 U. S. 443.   The State of Virginia had found it necessary to pass even more stringent laws to prevent the taxpayers from forcing their claims. An English brokerage establishment had bought $100,000 worth of those coupons, in London, buying them for about $30,000, for the purpose of selling them to the taxpayers of Virginia, of course at an increase upon cost, but at a price below face value. To meet this move, the State, by statute, established additional restrictions to be complied with before the coupons could be accepted for taxes,—acts passed, of course, under the guise of means to detect counterfeit coupons. There were two chief characteristics of these laws: First, in order to make the coupon receivable the one who owned it had to be able to present the original bond from which it was cut; secondly, no expert evidence was allowed in the court to verify the coupons, that is, no attorney could be employed. Thus by the various acts in question the State had forced the taxpayers "into a lawsuit in her own courts, in which she has taken effectual precaution beforehand to make it impossible they can win." Such legislation the plaintiffs contended to be an impairment of the obligation of the State's contracts. Pressed to the wall by this contention, the officers of the State pleaded that the suit against them was a suit against the State and hence could not be maintained. This the United States Supreme Court held to be the case.

Justice Harlan, of course, did not approve this decision any more than he had approved that of Antoni v. Greenhow. He said: "The commonwealth of Virginia has no more authority to enact statutes impairing the obligation of her contracts than statutes impairing the obligation of contracts exclusively between individuals. . . . A statute which is void, as impairing the obligation of the State's contract, affords no justification to anyone, and confers no authority. If an officer proposes to enforce such a statute against a party, the obligation of whose contract is sought to be impaired, the latter, in my judgment, may proceed, by suit, against such officer, and thereby obtain protection in his rights of contract, as against the proposed action of that officer. A contrary view enables the State to use her immunity from suit to effect what the Constitution of the United States forbids her from doing; namely, to enact statutes impairing the obligation of contracts."

Another case wherein Justice Harlan differed from the court in its interpretation of the contract clause in the Constitution of the United States is that of Louisiana v. Mayor, etc., of New Orleans, 109 U. S. 285. This case was long and much involved. It will be treated again under due process of law, but the matter of contract was discussed by both Justice Harlan and the court.

The State of Louisiana had passed a law making the county or town in which property had been destroyed by mob violence responsible for the value of such property destroyed. The State had by a later statute forbidden cities to levy taxes above a certain percentage. Private property of a considerable amount had been destroyed in New Orleans by mob violence. The party whose property had been destroyed brought suit against the city of New Orleans for the value of the property destroyed, and obtained judgment for the amount. The city refused to pay the judgment, asserting that within the bounds of the percentage allowed under the subsequent statute of the State she had collected all the money collectable and had no funds with which to pay the judgment. The question was, did the subsequent law of Louisiana, which held the city within certain limits in making assessments, amount to an impairment of the obligation of contracts, in that it deprived citizens of what had been guaranteed to them by the previous law? The court said that it did not, but Justice Harlan said that it did. His contention, however, was more vigorous on the point of due process of law than on that of contract, although the court dwelt mainly upon the contract feature. It must be admitted that this would have been a rather far-fetched interpretation of the word contract. But here, as in the above cases, Justice Harlan seemed to feel that the city was, by means of a technicality, slipping out of an obligation imposed upon it by the State. This sort of dishonesty always aroused his indignation.

Of the general ability of a State to impair contract clauses in charters seemingly permanent in their scope there is one very interesting case, Stone v. Farmers' Loan and Trust Co., 116 U. S. 307. It was brought from the United States circuit court for the southern district of Mississippi in order to test the validity of a state statute establishing a railroad commission to examine and pass upon tariffs and other railroad regulations. In chartering the railroad company the State of Mississippi embodied the following stipulation in its charter: "That the president and directors be and they are hereby authorized to adopt and establish such a tariff of charges for the transportation of persons and property as they may think proper, and the same to alter and change at pleasure." The contention of the railroad company was that the statute establishing a commission to regulate the tariffs was an impairment of the obligation of contracts in that it took from the company the power granted in the original charter to fix its own rates.

The import of the decision amounted to this: The fact that the railroad company had been granted the right to fix rates did not imply that the State might not also exercise that power. Since the State was not forbidden by the contract to fix rates, the establishment of a commission for that purpose did not impair the obligation of contracts. It implied that though the company might fix any rate it pleased, the commission could also do so, and that the latter rate was the only one that could be enforced in the courts.

Justice Harlan thought differently. He contended that the statute in question did constitute an impairment of the obligation of contracts and was void. He held, however, that the railroad company could not establish any rate it pleased to establish, but that rates established by the railroad company should hold unless declared unreasonable by some competent court. He said: "I am of opinion that this statute impairs the obligation of the contract which the State made with these companies, in this: that it takes from each of them the power conferred by its charter, of fixing and regulating rates for transportation within the limit of reasonableness; and confers upon a commission authority to establish, from time to time, such rates as will give a fair and just return on the *value* of such railroad, its appurtenances and equipments, and as experience and business operations may show to be just. In short, the companies are placed by the statute in the same condition they would occupy if their charter had not conferred upon them the power to fix and regulate rates for transportation. The whole subject of transportation rates is thus remitted to the judgment of commissioners who have no pecuniary interest whatever in the management of these vast properties, and who, if they had any such interest, would be disqualified under the statute from serving; and who are required to fix rates, according to the value of the property, without any reference to what it originally cost or what it had cost to maintain it in fit condition for public use. . . .

"In expressing the foregoing views I would not be understood as denying the power of the State to establish a Railroad Commission, or to enforce regulations (not inconsistent with the essential charter rights of the companies) in reference to the general conduct of their merely local business. My only purpose is to express the conviction that each of these companies has a contract with the State, whereby it is exempted from absolute legislative control as to rates, and under which it may, through its directors, from time to time, within the limit of reasonableness, establish such rates of toll for the transportation of persons and property as they deem proper; such rates to be respected by the courts and by the public, unless they are shown affirmatively to be unreasonable."

Justice Harlan's contention in this case is not inconsistent, as may be thought, with some of his later dissents regarding the power of the Interstate Commerce Commission. He impliedly recognized here that the State may establish a commission of this kind without unconstitutional delegation of the legislative power, an assertion which he made more vigorously in his dissent from Interstate Commerce Commission v. Alabama Midland R. Co., 168 U. S. 144. Neither was his doctrine as inexpedient as might be thought. He wished to have the State keep its word, and at the same time give the railroads to understand that their rates must be in accordance with reason. Yet it must be admitted that from the point of view of facility in the regulation of railroad rates the decision of the court was wiser.[1]

From the cases discussed may be deduced Justice Harlan's doctrine regarding the relation of a State to its own contract. It was merely this: that a State could, constitutionally, no more impair its own contracts than it could impair any other contracts; and that necessary proceedings should have been taken to prevent the States from impairing their own contracts.

Relation of the National Government to its Contracts.— As is well known, there is no constitutional limitation directly forbidding the United States to pass laws impairing the obligation of contracts. Though the national government has not been very careful not to impair the obligation of contracts, yet, when suits have been brought on this question, the court has argued that the action was not an impairment.

Justice Harlan held that, though there was no express statement to that effect in the Constitution, the stipulations

---

[1] With regard to land grants there is one case, and in that the difference was rather technical, involving the interpretation of the meaning of the terms of the contract. This was the case of Walsh v. Preston, 109 U. S. 297. The court decided that if a State grants land on contract, and if within good time the party to whom the land was granted cannot show that he has complied with the contract, the land is subject to regrantal. Justice Harlan differed from the court in that he contended that the party to whom the land was granted had given sufficient evidence of having complied with his part of the contract, and that the State had impaired the obligation of its contract in regranting any part of the land.

that property should not be taken without due process of law, and particularly that private property should not be taken without just compensation, implied that the obligation of contracts could not be impaired. This question came up particularly in the cases involving the rights of patentees. There are three cases of special interest: Schillinger v. United States, 155 U. S. 163; Belknap v. Schild, 161 U. S. 10; and International Postal Supply Co. v. Bruce, 194 U. S. 601. These have been alluded to in the preceding chapter, but may be considered here in their relation to contracts.

The first of these cases came before the Supreme Court on the plea that a paving company, employed by the government at Washington, had used a patented process in employing tarred paper to keep cement blocks apart, and had thus impaired an implied contract right of the patentee to the exclusive use of his patented invention. The court decided that this use did not constitute an impairment of the obligation of contracts and that it was not a contract relation, but that the injury alleged was in the nature of a tort, and no action could be had against the United States for it. "So not only does the petition count upon a tort, but also the findings show a tort. That is the essential fact underlying the transaction and upon which rests every pretense of a right to recover. There was no suggestion of a waiver of the tort or a pretence of any implied contract until after the decision of the Court of Claims that it had no jurisdiction over an action to recover for the tort."

Justice Harlan, however, thought otherwise. With him, the United States government, in granting patents, formed contracts which it could not impair any more than could a state impair the obligation of its contracts. Some quotations will illustrate this point. " It may, therefore, be regarded as settled that the government may be sued in the Court of Claims, as upon implied contract, not only for the value of specific property taken for public use by an officer acting under the authority of the government, even if the taking was originally without the consent of the owner and without legal proceedings for condemnation, but for the value of the use of a patented invention when such use was with the consent of the patentee. . . .

"If Schillinger's patent was valid, then the government is bound by an obligation of the highest character to compensate him for the use of his invention, and its use by the government cannot be said to arise out of mere tort, at least when its representative did not himself dispute, nor assume to decide, the validity of the patent. If the Act of Congress under which the architect proceeded had, in express terms, directed him to use Schillinger's invention in any pavement laid down in the public grounds, then such use, according to the decision in *United States* v. *Great Falls Mfg. Co.*, would have made a case of implied contract based on the constitutional obligation to make just compensation for private property taken for public use. But such a case is not distinguishable, in principle, from the present one, where the architect, proceeding under a general authority to expend the public money according to specified plans, uses or knowingly permits to be used a particular patented invention, not disputing the rights of the patentee, but leaving the question of the validity of the patent, and the consequent liability of the government for its use, to judicial determination."

The case of Belknap v. Schild was sufficiently explained in the chapter on suability of States. In his dissent from this case Justice Harlan reiterated his arguments in Schillinger v. United States, but somewhat more vehemently: "If the United States may appropriate to public use the invention of a patentee, without his consent, and without liability to suit, as upon implied contract, for the value of the use of such invention; if, as the court holds, a public officer acting only in the interest of the public is not individually liable for gains, profits, and advantages that may accrue to the United States from such use; and if the officer who thus violates the rights of the patentee cannot be restrained by injunction,—then the government may well be

regarded as organized robbery so far as the rights of patentees are concerned."

The details of the case of the International Postal Supply
Co. v. Bruce have also been sufficiently explained. Here
Justice Harlan, more vigorously than ever, reasserted the
convictions expressed in the former dissents: "It is now
adjudged that, although a postmaster may be confessedly
proceeding in direct violation of the legal rights of the patentee, the court cannot, by any direct process, stop him in
his destruction of the patentee's right of property. Under
the present decision, the Postoffice Department not only
may use, without compensation, the particular postmarking
machines in question here, but it can lease others, and continue its violation of the patentee's rights at its discretion,
thereby making the exclusive use granted by the patent of
no value whatever."

From these opinions it is seen that, though there is no
express prohibition upon the United States forbidding the
impairment of the obligation of contracts, yet, according to
Justice Harlan's doctrine, the prohibitions as to taking private property without just compensation and without due
process of law would have worked to that end. But his
doctrine did not prevail, and as the decisions now stand, the
United States may impair the obligation of what in substance would appear to be contracts.

The Relation of a Foreign Government to Contracts.—
Justice Harlan held also that a foreign government could
not pass laws which the United States need recognize by international comity.   This theory is brought out in his dissent in Canada Southern R. Co. v. Gebhard, 109 U. S. 527.
A railroad company chartered in Canada had, in 1871, made
a bond issue which was to pay seven per cent interest, to be
collected in New York, the bonds to mature in 1906.   In
1873 the company found it impossible to pay the interest
on the coupons, and made a new issue of bonds, stipulating
that the principal and interest should be paid within a short
time, also in New York, thus making possible the payment

of interest on the coupons of the former issue. Upon the maturity of the second bond issue the company was unable to meet its obligations. To remedy the situation the Parliament of Canada passed a statute providing for the surrender of the old bonds, bearing seven per cent interest, and the substitution of other bonds, maturing at a later date, and bearing a less rate of interest. The case was fought out in the United States circuit court, where the decision was that such a statute was an impairment of the obligation of contracts, and a judgment was issued against the railroad company. Upon appeal to the Supreme Court, the decision of the lower court was reversed. The reasons for the decree of the court were these: In the first place, the statute of Canada was in the nature of bankruptcy or foreclosure proceedings, and was not different in purpose from similar proceedings here; and, in the second place, international comity made it necessary that the United States recognize the validity of the act of the Canadian Parliament.

Neither of these contentions met with Justice Harlan's approval. He claimed that the proceeding was significantly different from bankruptcy or foreclosure proceedings in that the creditors had not been allowed their day in court. "It is unlike a composition in bankruptcy in this: that whereas a composition is never had except upon notice, so that creditors may have their day in court, with opportunity to show that the proposed composition should not be made, here, no such opportunity was given to the holders of this company's bonds, in any court or other tribunal, to show that the arrangement which the Canadian Parliament sanctioned ought not, in justice, to be made; but the arrangement was, by legislative enactment, made absolutely binding upon every bondholder and stockholder, even those who are citizens of other countries." To the second contention he objected that it was not fair to allow Canada to deny to American citizens what the American government could deny neither to them nor to citizens of Canada. "In this country, no State can pass any law impairing the obligation of contracts; the Constitution of the United States forbids such legislation. And the principle is founded in justice, independently of this constitutional provision. . . . A citizen of Canada, or even a railway corporation of that Dominion, could have the benefit, in our courts, of the constitutional inhibition upon state laws impairing the obligation of contracts."

The conclusion is as follows: "As I do not think that a foreign railway corporation is entitled, upon principles of international comity, to have the benefit, in our courts—to the prejudice of our own people and in violation of their contract and property rights—of a foreign statute which could not be sustained had it been enacted by Congress or by any one of the United States, with reference to the negotiable securities of an American railway corporation; and as I do not agree that an American court should accord to a foreign railway corporation the privilege of repudiating its contract obligations to American citizens, when it must deny any such privilege, under like circumstances, to our own railway corporations, I dissent from the opinion and judgment of the court."

It is seen, therefore, that according to Justice Harlan's doctrine the United States need not recognize that a foreign government has any more right to pass laws impairing the obligation of contracts of American citizens than has the home government.

To sum up Justice Harlan's doctrine of the obligation of contracts: He believed that the enforcement of valid contracts was a right to which all people were entitled and that the right lay deeper than any express command or limitation, being founded in abstract justice. Holding this view, he would not give his assent to any state law that impaired the obligation of contracts, and he thought that the necessary proceedings should always have been taken to prevent any impairment of state contracts, whether in regard to the State's own contracts or those of private citizens. Moreover, he contended with equal vigor that there was just as sacred a duty on the part of the United States not to impair in any way the obligation of legal contracts.   Furthermore, he thought that the courts of the United States should always pronounce against the recognition of the right of any foreign government to impair contracts of the citizens of the United States, in the same way in which they would or should oppose such impairment here.

CHAPTER III

DUE PROCESS OF LAW

Just as it is practically impossible to get an exact and final definition of the expression "due process of law" to fit the general study of constitutional law, so it is difficult to state positively what any one person has conceived it to be. Justice Harlan has in several places set forth decided opinions as to this conception. As he was inclined to be strongly nationalistic in his tendencies, one would suppose that he would have wanted to give it a broader interpretation than the court as a whole has found it fitting to do. This, however, is not entirely true. In some respects he did wish to make the meaning broader than the court had decided, but in the majority of cases his view was a more limited one.

Before taking up the various instances in which he has differed from the court and in which his decided convictions on this subject will be in the foreground, some quotations illustrative of his general doctrine will be given.

In his dissent from Hurtado v. California, 110 U. S. 516, he gives the following quotation from a former decision[1] as expressing his opinion: "The Constitution contains no description of those processes which it was intended to allow or forbid. It does not even declare what principles are to be applied to ascertain whether it be due process. It is manifest that it was not left to the legislative power to enact any process which might be devised. The article is a restraint on the legislative as well as on the executive and judicial powers of the government, and cannot be so construed as to leave Congress free to make any process 'due process of law' by its mere will. To what principles are

---
[1] Murray v. Land and Improvement Co., 18 How. 272.

we to resort to ascertain whether this process enacted by
Congress is due process? To this the answer must be
twofold. We must examine the Constitution itself to see
whether this process be in conflict with any of its provisions.
If not found to be so, we must look *to those settled usages
and modes of proceeding existing in the common and statute law of England before the emigration of our ancestors,
and which are shown not to have been unsuited to their
civil and political condition by having been acted on by them
after the settlement of this country."*

According to this opinion, to ascertain whether any legislation or any governmental act of any kind is contrary to
the prohibition in the Constitution as to due process of law,
two questions must be asked: First, is there any other provision in the Constitution which forbids it? If so, it is, of
course, not due process of law. Secondly, do the customs
and practices of English law forbid? If so, it is not due
process. Though the first criterion is definite, the second
may give rise to much dispute. According to Justice Harlan, however, these criteria furnish safe guides in ascer-
taining whether any act is constitutional within the meaning
of that clause of the fourteenth amendment.

A quotation from Justice Harlan's dissent in the Hurtado
case will show his position: "'Due process of law,' within
the meaning of the national constitution, does not import
one thing with reference to the powers of the States, and
another with reference to the powers of the general government. If particular proceedings conducted under the
authority of the general government, and involving life,
are prohibited, because not constituting that due process of
law required by the 5th Amendment of the Constitution
of the United States, similar proceedings, conducted under
the authority of a State, must be deemed illegal as not being
due process of law within the meaning of the 14th Amendment." As will be shown presently, the court has not held
to this view. But it is a strange sort of interpretation,
according to Justice Harlan, which explains due process

differently for two different spheres of government under the same constitution.

Another quotation, from Justice Harlan's dissent from Taylor v. Beckham, 178 U. S. 548, will be appropriate here: "The liberty of which the 14th Amendment forbids a state from depriving anyone without due process of law is something more than freedom from the enslavement of the body or from physical restraint. In my judgment the words 'life, liberty, or property' in the 14th Amendment should be interpreted as embracing every right that may be brought within judicial cognizance, and therefore no right of that kind can be taken in violation of 'due process of law.'"

Life and Liberty.—The question of deprivation of life or liberty without due process of law involves mainly the matter of criminal procedure. In fact, Justice Harlan's doctrine appears most clearly in his dissents from cases involving trial by jury,—cases in which trial by jury has been limited. The first and chief case on this subject was that of Hurtado v. California, 110 U. S. 516.

This case involved an indictment without grand jury of a person who was accused of murder. The case was taken to the Supmere Court of the United States, on the ground that the statute of California which allowed such a procedure was unconstitutional in that it deprived the criminal of his life without due process of law. The question for the court to decide, then, was whether denial of indictment by grand jury constituted a denial of due process of law.

The decision in this case was delivered by Justice Matthews, and his arguments may be summarized as follows: (1) Referring to the test for due process of law as given in Murray v. Land and Improvement Co., quoted above, he said that this is not the only test for due process of law. "This, it is argued, furnishes an indispensable test of what constitutes 'due process of law'; that any proceeding otherwise authorized by law, which is not thus sanctioned by usage, or which supersedes and displaces one that is, cannot be regarded as due process of law.

"But this inference is unwarranted. The real syllabus of the passage quoted is, that a process of law, which is not otherwise forbidden, must be taken to be due process of law, if it can show the sanction of settled usage both in England and in this country; but it by no means follows, that nothing else can be due process of law. The point in the case cited arose in reference to a summary proceeding, questioned on that account, as not due process of law. . . . But to hold that such a characteristic is essential to due process of law, would be to deny every quality of the law but its age, and to render it incapable of progress or improvement. It would be to stamp upon our jurisprudence the unchangeableness attributed to the laws of the Medes and Persians." This declaration is reenforced with the statement that such a principle might require trial by ordeal. (2) Since the words "due process of law" were used in the fifth amendment in connection with the constitutional guarantee of trial by jury, and in the fourteenth without this guarantee, it may be taken that this omission gives room for allowing the States to abandon jury trials. "If in the adoption of that Amendment it had been part of its purpose to perpetuate the institution of the grand jury in all the States, it would have embodied, as did the 5th Amendment, express declarations to that effect. Due process of law in the latter refers to that law of the land, which derives its authority from the legislative powers conferred upon Congress by the Constitution of the United States, exercised within the limits therein prescribed, and interpreted according to the principles of the common law. In the 14th Amendment, by parity of reason, it refers to that law of the land in each State, which derives its authority from the inherent and reserved powers of the State, exerted within the limits of those fundamental principles of liberty and justice which lie at the base of all our civil and political institutions, and the greatest security for which resides in the right of the people to make their own laws, and alter them at their pleasure."

It is seen that the contention of the court was that the institution in cases of felonies of a procedure other than jury trial did not abridge a right guaranteed by the Constitution because, in the first place, due process of law might mean more than had been previously recognized as proper procedure, otherwise progress in criminal procedure would be thwarted. In the second place, since the provision regarding due process of law as given in the fourteenth amendment was inserted without a special stipulation regarding jury trial, it could not be taken to mean that trial by jury was necessary. Then follows this definition of due process of law: " It follows that any legal proceeding enforced by public authority, whether sanctioned by age and custom, or newly devised in the discretion of the legislative power, in furtherance of the general public good, which regards and preserves these principles of liberty and justice, must be held to be due process of law."

These contentions did not meet Justice Harlan's approval. In answer to the first argument of the court he showed that usage and custom both in England and in the United States required that criminal cases be tried only by a jury. In addition to the fact that this requirement had been made in the Constitution of the United States, it had been made in the constitution of practically every State. A custom which had received such sanction was not to be lightly brushed aside as a relic of barbarism. In other words, it was so predominant a characteristic as to require a constitutional amendment before it could be done away with anywhere in the United States.

In answer to the second contention of the court the following argument was made by Justice Harlan: "This line of argument, it seems to me, would lead to results which are inconsistent with the vital principles of republican government. If the presence in the 5th Amendment of a specific provision for grand juries in capital cases, alongside the provision for due process of law in proceedings involving life, liberty or property, is held to prove that due process of law did not, in the judgment of the framers of the Constitution, necessarily require a grand jury in capital cases, inexorable logic would require it to be, likewise, held that the right not to be put twice in jeopardy of life and limb for the same offense, nor compelled in a criminal case to testify against one's self (rights and immunities also specifically recognized in the 5th Amendment) were not protected by that due process of law required by the settled usages and proceedings existing under the common and statute law of England at the settlement of this country. More than that, other Amendments of the Constitution proposed at the same time, expressly recognize the right of persons to just compensation for private property taken for public use; their right, when accused of crime, to be informed of the nature and cause of the accusation against them, and to a speedy and public trial, by an impartial jury of the State and district wherein the crime was committed; to be confronted by the witnesses against them; and to have compulsory process for obtaining witnesses in their favor. . . . If the argument of my brethren be sound, those rights (although universally recognized at the establishment of our institutions as secured by that due process of law which for centuries had been the foundation of Anglo-Saxon liberty) were not deemed by our fathers as essential in the due process of law prescribed by our Constitution; because—such seems to be the argument—had they been regarded as involved in due process of law, they would not have been specifically and expressly provided for, but left to the protection given by the general clause forbidding the deprivation of life, liberty or property without due process of law. . . .

" So that the court, in this case, while conceding that the requirement of due process of law protects the fundamental principles of liberty and justice, adjudges, in effect, that an immunity or right, recognized at the common law to be essential to personal security, jealously guarded by our National Constitution against violation by any tribunal or body exercising authority under the General Government, and expressly or impliedly recognized, *when the 14th Amendment was adopted,* in the Bill of Rights or Constitution of every State in the Union, is yet, not a fundamental principle in governments established, as those of the States of the Union are, to secure to the citizen liberty and justice and, therefore, is not involved in that due process of law required in proceedings conducted under the sanction of a State."[2]

The case of Hurtado v. California seems to be the most significant case in which there is an answer to the question as to the relation of due process of law to trial by jury. There is no express constitutional stipulation that a State shall not deprive persons of the right of trial by jury; hence, if a State does enact a law which denies this right to its citizens, the only constitutional stipulation under which the law may be tested by the Supreme Court of the United States is that in the fourteenth amendment which says that life, liberty, or property shall not be denied by a State to any person without due process of law. When the question as to the denial of the right of trial by jury has been contested under the laws of the United States proper, the plaintiffs have preferred to bring up the cases under the express limitation upon the United States that jury trial shall not be denied.

The cases of Hawaii v. Mankichi, 190 U. S. 197, and Schick v. United States, 195 U. S. 65, are typical cases in this connection. The first will be discussed under the topic of judicial legislation[3] and in the comments upon the Insular Cases,[4] and may be omitted here. Although the case of Schick v. United States cannot be said to bear directly upon the question of due process of law, it can best be discussed here as illustrative of Justice Harlan's belief that

---

[2] See Thompson v. Utah, 170 U. S. 343, where Justice Harlan in rendering the majority opinion stated that criminal procedure must be by jury trial in all territories of the United States.

[3] See pages 197–198.

[4] See pages 185–188.

trial by jury is a fundamental doctrine, and one not to be dealt with lightly, as the court has at times showed a tendency to do.

The question to be settled in this case was whether a man accused of crime could waive trial by jury. The plaintiffs in error had been prosecuted after a trial by information in a district court of the United States for violation of a national law which required that oleomargarine should be stamped in a certain way. The court held that since the fine could not exceed fifty dollars, this was a petty offense, and hence was not meant to be included within the third article, which states that " the trial of all crimes, except in cases of impeachment, shall be by jury." The argument was (1) that the clause did not necessarily embrace offenses like this one. In support of this assertion the court went into the history of the clause. The fact that the constitutional convention had changed the phrase " criminal procedure " to the word " crimes " argued in the mind of the court that the word crimes was meant to embrace only those of deeper significance. (2) If a man guilty of murder may, by pleading guilty and throwing himself upon the mercy of the court, do away with trial by jury, why could not one informed against for a petty offense waive the trial by jury?

In dissenting in this case Justice Harlan showed that the whole wording of the act went to show that all crimes were meant to be included within its scope, and that history did not bear out any other interpretation of the requirement in the Constitution that trial by jury should be always upheld. Since, therefore, every consideration went to show that the charge in question was a crime within the meaning of both the statute and the Const tution, the only legal mode of procedure was that of trial by jury. He thereupon proceeded to examine the bearing of history on that particular case, and found that nothing in the practices of English law justified the trial of such a case in any other way.

His answer to the contention of the court that the plain-

tiff had a right to waive trial by jury is well worth quoting:
" In this connection we are confronted with the broad statement, found in some adjudged cases as well as in elemen-
tary treatises, to the effect that a person is entitled to waive
any constitutional right, of whatever nature, that he pos-
sesses, and thereby preclude himself from invoking the
authority of the Constitution for the protection or enforcement of that right. It is suggested that even when charged
with murder he may plead guilty, and that the court thereupon, without the intervention of a jury, may pronounce
such judgment as the law permits or authorizes. And it is
confidently asked by those who make that suggestion, Why
may not one charged with a misdemeanor, and pleading not
guilty, waive a jury altogether, and consent to be tried by
the court? This argument will not stand the test of reason.
It proceeds upon the ground that jurisdiction to try a criminal case may be given by consent of the accused and the
prosecutor. But such consent could have no legal efficacy.
Undoubtedly one accused of murder may plead guilty. But
in doing so he renders a trial unnecessary. The Constitution does not prohibit an accused from pleading guilty.
His right to do so was recognized long before the adoption
of that instrument; and it was never supposed that such a
plea impaired the force of the requirement that a trial for
crime, under a plea of not guilty, shall be by jury. It is not
to be assumed that the Constitution intended, when pre-
serving the right of trial by jury, to change any essential
rule of criminal practice established at the common law,
before the adoption of the instrument. When the accused
pleads guilty before a lawful tribunal he admits every material fact well averred in the indictment or information,
and there is no issue to be tried; no facts are to be found;
no trial occurs. After such a plea nothing remains to be
done except that the court shall pronounce judgment upon
the facts voluntarily confessed by the accused. What the Constitution requires is that the *trial* of a crime shall be by jury.
If the accused pleads not guilty, there must, of necessity,

be a trial; for by that plea he puts 'himself on his country, which country the jury are'; he contests, by that plea, every fact necessary to establish his guilt; he is presumed to be innocent; nothing is confessed; and the facts necessary to show guilt must be judicially ascertained, in the mode prescribed by law, before any judgment can be rendered."

Justice Harlan's answer to the contention of the court that a man may waive trial by jury is based upon the fact that he had not pleaded guilty. If he has pleaded guilty, of course, as Justice Harlan said, there will be no need for trial; the case is determined, and the only thing that remains to be done is to administer the penalty. In other words, the jury is to determine whether a man is guilty or innocent, when he pleads not guilty. This is the only method allowed by the Constitution. Justice Harlan's constitutional doctrine is that the only process of law by which a man may be deprived of his life or liberty is by complete jury trial, according to the customary meaning; and so long as the Constitution reads as it does, there is no other recourse, either for the government or for the accused.

Property.—The court has in many cases been called on to determine what is and what is not property, and has pronounced some things not to be property which Justice Harlan thought ought to be considered such; but it cannot be said that it has declared anything to be property which he thought ought not to be so considered. There are several interesting cases bearing on this point. The case of Louisiana v. Mayor, etc., of New Orleans, 109 U. S. 285, was an early one in Justice Harlan's experience.

The case involved a statute of Louisiana which made the locality in which mob violence had been the cause of destruction of property responsible for such destruction. The case has been explained in the chapter on the obligation of contracts.[5] A judgment having been secured against the city of New Orleans for property destroyed, the city re-

---

[5] See page 49.

fused to make payment, on the ground that there were insufficient funds in the treasury, and that it was impossible, under the statute of Louisiana which limited the amount of assessment, to collect taxes to meet this obligation. The question was, did this later statute, which prohibited an assessment beyond a certain percentage, deprive the person who held the judgment of his property without due process of law? The court, speaking through Justice Field, did not answer this question exactly in the negative, but gave an answer which amounted to the same thing.

The discussion by the court of this point is very brief. Justice Harlan, however, in his dissent dwells on it at length. The court spoke as follows: "Conceding that the judgments, though founded upon claims to indemnity for unlawful acts of mobs or riotous assemblages, are property in the sense that they are capable of ownership and may have a pecuniary value, the relators cannot be said to be deprived of them so long as they continue an existing liability against the city. Although the present limitation of the taxing power of the city may prevent the receipt of sufficient funds to pay the judgment, the Legislature of the State may, upon proper appeal, make other provisions for their satisfaction. The judgment may also perhaps be used by the relators or their assignees as offsets to demands of the city; at least it is possible that they may be available in various ways. Be this as it may, the relators have no such vested right in the taxing power of the city as to render its diminution by the State, to a degree affecting the present collection of their judgments, a deprivation of their property in the sense of the constitutional prohibition. A party cannot be said to be deprived of his property in a judgment because at the time he is unable to collect it."

This gives in full the bearing of the opinion upon the point of due process of law. The main part of the opinion is devoted to showing that the statute in question did not impair the obligation of contracts. The question of due process, which Justice Harlan thought ought to have determined the case for the plaintiffs, was therefore slurred over. It is seen that the argument was not that the judgments were not property, but that they were not property in the sense that their immediate collection could be forced.

The contention of the court on this point did not suit Justice Harlan. He knew that there were ulterior motives behind the plea of the city that there was no money in its treasury to meet these obligations. To him these judgments constituted a just debt which ought to be paid. He therefore undertook to prove that judgments are property, and that the statute was unconstitutional in that it deprived the owner of their enforcement. "Its value as property depends in every legal sense upon the remedies which the law gives to enforce its collection. To withhold from the citizen who has a judgment for money, the judicial means of enforcing its collection; or, what is, in effect, the same thing, to withdraw from the judgment debtor, a municipal corporation, the authority to levy taxes for its payment, is to destroy the value of the judgment as property. . . . If the property of the citizen is ' taken,' within the meaning of the Constitution, when its value is destroyed or permanently impaired through the act of the government, or by the acts of others under the sanction or authority of the government, it would seem that the citizen holding a judgment for money against a municipal corporation—which judgment is capable of enforcement by judicial proceedings at the time of its rendition—is deprived of his property without due process of law, if the State, by a subsequent law, so reduces the rate of taxation as to make it impossible for the corporation to satisfy such judgment. Since the value of the judgment, as property, depends necessarily upon the remedies given for its enforcement, the withdrawal of all remedies for its enforcement, and compelling the owner to rely exclusively upon the generosity of the judgment debtor, is, I submit, to deprive the owner of his property."

In reply to the contention of the court that the judgments were still existing liabilities against the city, Justice Harlan said: "My answer is, that such liability on the part of the city is of no consequence, unless, when payment is refused, it can be enforced by legal proceedings."

Another case which involved a somewhat similar consideration came up from West Virginia. It was the case of Freeland v. Williams, 131 U. S. 405, and was a question of trespass which took place during the Civil War. Freeland while a soldier had taken cattle from Williams. Williams sued Freeland and received judgment. After this proceeding, a new constitution went into effect for West Virginia, a section of which relieved persons of such debts incurred during the Civil War. One of the questions was, did that section of the constitution of West Virginia which made it impossible for Williams to collect the money on his judgment take property without due process of law? The court, speaking through Justice Miller, said that it did not. Justice Harlan in his dissent said that it did.

'In giving the reasons for its decision, the court spoke as follows: "Was it competent for that convention to establish a rule of law which is now the recognized rule of this court, and perhaps of all the courts of the United States, which is commended by the highest authorities, and which is eminently adapted to the purpose of quieting strife and securing repose after the turmoils of a civil war, although the principle asserted was in opposition to that held by the supreme court of appeals of the State? That this principle would govern all cases where the act for which the party was sued occurred after its establishment does not admit of question. That it was the law of the country before its adoption by the State constitution there is as little doubt. Shall it be held to be incapable of enforcement and forbidden by the Constitution of the United States because it is made to cover judgments already rendered in violation of the principle asserted? The Constitution of the State remedies the defects of the proceeding by bill in chancery; it creates no new process of law; it makes that which always has been due process of law efficient by removing objections and obstructions to its operation. It simply declares that a judgment for a wrong or tort, which in itself was erroneous, is a voidable judgment, and may be voided, if it can be brought within due process of law already existing, and shall by this means be inquired into, and if it is against right, justice, and law, shall be no longer in force, and the judgment plaintiff shall be forever enjoined from putting it into execution." Thus it is seen that the argument of the court amounts to saying that it is not unconstitutional for a State so to amend its constitution as to take property as long as the means through which that property is taken are not in conflict with a process of law which has become widely recognized as due process of law.

Justice Harlan could not accept that doctrine. In his dissent is found the following opinion: " If the taking of cattle was illegal, the right to recover from the wrong-doer their reasonable value was an absolute one, of which the owner could not be deprived by a legislative enactment of the State, or by an amendment of its Constitution. The judgment obtained by Freeland was an adjudication that the taking was illegal. He acquired by that judgment a vested right to have and demand the amount named in it, as well as the benefit of such remedies as the law gave for the enforcement of personal judgments for money. The judgment was, therefore, property of which the State could not deprive him, except by due process of law. And a constitutional provision, subsequently enacted, declaring that the defendant's property should not be seized or sold under final process on such judgment, is not due process of law. I cannot agree that a State may, by amendment of its fundamental law, prevent a citizen from recovering the value of property, of which, according to the final judgment of its own courts, he has been illegally deprived by a mere trespasser. That would be sheer spoliation under the forms of law. If the amendment in question had, in terms, given the defendant a right to a new trial, of the action of trespass in the same court, after the time had passed, within which, according to the settled modes of procedure, he could, of right, apply for a new trial, it would have accomplished, in respect to the judgment against him, precisely what, in effect, has been held by this court to be consistent with the Fourteenth Amendment. . . .

"The only possible ground upon which the judgment below can be sustained, consistently with the law of the land, is to hold that no court of any State had any jurisdiction in the year 1867, even with the parties before it, to inquire, in any action of trespass, whether an alleged taking of the private property of a citizen was a mere trespass, or was an act of war upon the part of the defendant, a Confederate soldier, and to give judgment according to the result of that inquiry."

From the above cases it may be deduced that Justice Harlan considered a judgment as property within the meaning of the Constitution of the United States, and held that any action taken by the State to render ineffective the collection of such judgment amounts to the taking of property without due process of law. It is true that the court did not hold that a judgment was not property, but it did hold that the action on the part of the State did not amount to the taking of property without due process of law. Since, however, the action of the State destroyed the value of the judgment in the hands of the owner, Justice Harlan contended that property had been taken. No doubt the court felt that a certain conclusion had to be reached, and that it was merely a matter of making the decision appear constitutional, or rather of seeming to justify an act as constitutional. Justice Harlan did not hold with such reasoning; with him the Constitution was too sacred for such twisting. The decision of the court may have been wise, but a contrary decision could certainly have done little to stir up any additional animosity.

The case of Backus v. Fort Street Union Depot Co., 169 U. S. 557, involved a somewhat complicated question of procedure. The contention between the court and Justice Harlan, however, was on the definite point of taking property without due process of law. The case came up from the supreme court of Michigan. The plea had been made that in a jury trial to determine what should be just compensation for property condemned for public use, just compensation had not been given because the judge had not properly charged the jury.

The condemnation was of a factory site, and the plaintiffs claimed that they should have had, in addition to the value of the property taken, the profits which they lost by changing the location of their factory, that is, during the time consumed by this change. The court said that the finding of the jury was due process of law, and that hence no property was unduly taken.

No particular argument needs to be noticed. The court said that it was due process, and Justice Harlan said that it was not. He concluded as follows: "Without referring to other matters discussed at the bar and in the elaborate brief of counsel, I place my dissent from the opinion and judgment of the court upon the ground that the trial court committed error in its charge to the jury as to the principles which should guide them in determining the just compensation to which the plantiffs in error were entitled." There was little question that the plaintiffs had not received full compensation for their property rights, and Justice Harlan doubtless appreciated that fact.

One of the most interesting and hotly contested cases that ever came up to the Supreme Court for determination of the meaning of property in connection with its seizure without due process of law was that of Taylor v. Beckham, 178 U. S. 548. This case came up from the Supreme Court of Kentucky, and involved the question of the election of the governor of that State. The facts in the case were briefly as follows: Taylor and Marshall were the Republican candidates for the governorship and lieutenant-governorship respectively of Kentucky. Goebel and Beckham were the

Democratic candidates. According to the election returns, Taylor and Marshall, the Republican candidates, were elected. The Democratic candidates filed a protest and proceeded to contest the election. According to the constitution of the State, the method of settling a contested election is to select by lot a number of men from each house of the General Assembly, who are to investigate the election and report as to who was elected. This was done, and when the committee returned its decision, it was in favor of the Democrats. Soon thereafter Goebel was shot, supposedly by Taylor, or at his instigation. The fight was nevertheless continued by the candidate for the lieutenant-governorship, Beckham. The committee to investigate the election decided, seemingly without any formal investigation, that Goebel and Beckham had received the majority of the votes cast and were elected. But Taylor would not surrender the office to Beckham, whereupon the latter took the case into the state supreme court. There the decision was rendered in favor of Beckham. Taylor then carried his appeal to the Supreme Court of the United States, claiming that the action of the legislature is not making a fair investigation of the election returns, and of the supreme court of the State in rendering its decision against him, had deprived him of his property without due process of law. In connection with this claim was also set up the plea that the summary fashion in which the investigating committee had arrived at its decision amounted to a denial of the republican form of government. Justice Harlan did not dwell on that point as much as on the question of due process of law. The court dismissed the case for want of jurisdiction, upon the ground that a public office is not property within the meaning of the Constitution, and that the whole question was political.

Justice Harlan thought that the court ought to have taken jurisdiction and declared to whom the office belonged. He thought that the right to an office was property, the ownership of which could not be interfered with without due process of law. He said: "The majority of this court decide that an office held under the authority of a State cannot in any case be deemed property within the meaning of the 14th Amendment, and hence, it is now adjudged, the action of a state legislature or state tribunal depriving one of a state office—under whatever circumstances or by whatever mode the result is accomplished—cannot be regarded as inconsistent with the Constitution of the United States. Upon that ground the court declines to take jurisdiction of this writ of error. If the court had dismissed the writ, or affirmed the judgment upon the ground that there had been no violation of the principles constituting due process of law, its action would not have been followed by the evil results which, I think, must inevitably follow from the decision now rendered."

From this it appears that Justice Harlan did not base his objection to the decision so much upon the assertion that in this particular case one had been deprived of property without due process of law, as upon the assertion of the court that public office cannot under any circumstances be considered property. It is clear, however, that he thought a proper investigation of this case would have found that the one who held office was not the one who had received the majority of the votes. It might have been difficult for the court to find that there was not deprivation without due process of law if public office had been declared to be property, yet if it were property the question should have been answered.

Justice Harlan furthermore challenged the assertion that precedent gave no grounds for determining whether a man had been deprived of his office without due process of law. He found by an examination of former decisions that whenever the dispute had been between individuals, public office had been considered a property right, whereas when the dispute was between the individual and the State, it had not been considered a property right. In the case of Kennard v. Louisiana, ex rel. Morgan, 92 U. S. 480, he found that the court had determined this very point. The claim had been advanced in that case that the State, through her judiciary, had deprived Kennard of his office without due process of law. But the court took jurisdiction of the case and affirmed the judgment of the supreme court of Louisiana upon the ground that the requirement in the fourteenth amendment of due process of law had not been violated. With this case as a precedent, the court refused to dismiss the case of Foster v. Kansas, ex rel. Johnston, 111 U. S. 201, where the sole issue was as to the right of Foster to hold the office of county attorney. In the case of Boyd v. Nebraska, ex rel. Thayer, 143 U. S. 135, the court had removed Boyd from office as governor of Nebraska and put Thayer in his place. In the case of Wilson v. North Carolina, 169 U. S. 586, the court had again declared that under justifying circumstances it would investigate and determine who was rightly entitled to hold office. From these cases it is seen that the court was not without significant precedent to answer the question asked.

Justice Harlan, after reviewing these cases, said: " When the Fourteenth Amendment forbade any State from depriving any person of life, liberty, or property without due process of law, I had supposed that the intention of the people of the United States was to prevent the deprivation of any legal right in violation of the fundamental guarantees inhering in due process of law. The prohibitions of that Amendment, as we have often said, apply to all the instrumentalities of the state, to its legislative, executive, and judicial authorities; and therefore it has become a settled doctrine in the constitutional jurisprudence of this country that 'whoever by virtue of public position under a state government deprives another of property, life, or liberty without due process of law . . . violates the constitutional inhibition; and as he acts in the name and for the state, and is clothed with the state's power, his act is that of the state. This must be so, or [as we have often said] the constitutional prohibition has no meaning.' "

These quotations show sufficiently well the grounds upon which Justice Harlan based his arguments. He evidently felt that with an impartial tribunal such as he conceived it the duty of the court to be, one that would shut out all other considerations and decide each particular case by an honest application of reason to law, such an explanation of the due process clause would have been a healthful interpretation of the Constitution, for it might serve to counteract much trickery in state elections.

The difference between what Justice Harlan conceived to be due process of law with regard to the taxation of property and the opinion which has been established by the decisions of the court seems to have revolved around the single point of special assessments. In a series of cases involving this question Justice Harlan has held consistently to one doctrine, and he has characteristically asserted it whenever the question has come before the court.

Before discussing the cases involving the principle of special assessment, a brief consideration may be advisable of the case of Linford v. Ellison, 155 U. S. 503, in which Justice Harlan was apparently in favor of a tax which contained an element of the injustice imputed to the special assessments as interpreted by the Supreme Court. In this case the court dismissed a suit against the city of Kaysville, in the Territory of Utah, because the amount of money involved did not give jurisdiction. The dispute arose out of the sale of a wagon belonging to a farmer living away from the settled portions of the city, to obtain the sum of fifty dollars due under the tax levied by the city. The sale of the wagon was effected by James H. Linford, Jr., the tax collector, and the suit was instituted against him by Ephraim P. Ellison, whose wagon had been sold, under the plea that since his property was too far removed from the city to receive any benefit from being within the corporate limits, the city tax upon his land took property without due process of law. The territorial court sustained his plea, and refunded to Ellison the fifty dollars. The case was appealed to the Supreme Court of the United States by the tax collector for a determination of the question whether the tax took property without due process of law. The court dismissed the case, asserting that since the amount involved was less than five thousand dollars it did not have jurisdiction. Justice Harlan, however, dissented from the opinion. He asserted very emphatically that the Supreme Court was called upon to review an act of a subordinate governmental authority which had been accused of taking property without due process of law, and that even if the amount in dispute did not reach the sum of five thousand dollars it was nevertheless a question for the court to answer.

In this connection he said: "It is not disputed that the plaintiff's lands are within the limits of Kaysville, as defined by the act of the territorial legislature. It is conceded that the seizure of the plaintiff's wagon for the taxes on his lands was legal, if the statute of the territory was constitutional so far as it authorized taxes to be imposed on such lands within the defined limits of Kaysville, as were agricultural lands, namely, lands outside of the platted part of the city, which did not receive the benefits of the city government. I submit that there is no disputed question in the case, except that which involves the constitutional power of the territorial legislature, acting under the United States, to authorize the imposition of taxes for city purposes on lands situated as are those of the plaintiff. The facts were agreed and it is apparent that the parties intended to raise no question except as to the validity of the authority exercised by the territorial legislature in empowering the city of Kaysville to tax the lands here in question."

The case of Norwood v. Baker, 172 U. S. 269, in which Justice Harlan rendered the opinion of the court, contains the essence of his doctrine on the point of special assessment. This case involved an unusually expanded burden upon an individual, and, as Justice Harlan contended, was an instance of what might be continually occurring, though to a less degree, when the attempt is not made to fix by the benefit received the proportion of special assessment that persons affected should pay. Here the property condemned was a strip of land belonging to a Mrs. Baker. The compensation made for the piece of land was $2000. The special assessment upon the owner amounted to $2218.58. Thus the owner was given less for her land than she had to pay as a special assessment; in other words, the city was charging her $218.58 for taking her land. This the court, speaking through Justice Harlan, held to be taking property without due process of law. "In our judgment the exaction from the owner of private property for the cost of public improvement in substantial excess of the special benefit accruing to him is, *to the extent of such excess,* a taking . . . of private property for public use without compensation. We say 'substantial excess,' because exact equality of taxation is not always attainable, and for that reason the excess of cost over special benefits, unless it be of a material character, ought not to be regarded by a court of equity when its aid is invoked to restrain the enforcement of a special assessment." It is thus seen that Justice Harlan did not desire the impossible,—an exact apportionment of the assessment according to the benefits to be derived, but at least an attempt at justice.

As has been noted, this decision put an aspect of uncertainty upon the law, for prior to this time the so-called frontage rule had been the method of special assessment. When the case of French v. Barber Asphalt Paving Co., 181 U. S. 324, came before the court, the decision of Norwood v. Baker was apparently overturned. The later case came, by writ of error, from the supreme court of Missouri. Improvements had been made by the Barber Asphalt Paving Company on a certain avenue in Kansas City, Missouri. A special tax had been assessed upon the owners of lots abutting on this avenue, to help pay for the new pavements. To this end liens had been taken upon those lots to secure the tax. The paving company instituted a suit to enforce these liens so as to receive payment for the work done by them. The state supreme court decided in favor of the company. Thereupon an appeal was taken to the Supreme Court by French and others, owners of abutting lots, who asserted that such a tax amounted to the taking of property without due process of law. The Supreme Court affirmed the decision of the state court, and thus reasserted the validity of the frontage rule.

In dissenting from this opinion Justice Harlan reasserted the doctrine laid down in Norwood v. Baker, and criticized the court for not following the precedent set by that case. He furthermore accused the court of vagueness as to what consideration should guide it thereafter in deciding whether or not a special assessment amounts to the taking of property without due process of law. He contended more vigorously than ever that no special assessment made without inquiry as to the benefits to be received by the individual through the improvement should be upheld. In concluding he said: "In my opinion the judgment in the present case should be reversed upon the ground that the assessment in question was made under a statutory *rule* excluding all inquiry as to special benefits and requiring the property abutting on the avenue in question to meet the entire cost of paving it, even if such cost was in substantial excess of the special benefits accruing to it; leaving Kansas City to obtain authority to make a new assessment upon the abutting property for so much of the cost of paving as may be found upon due inquiry to be not in excess of the special benefits accruing to such property."

It may be judged from the above cases that Justice Harlan's constitutional doctrine as to the relation between special taxation and due process of law is that any special tax levied is unconstitutional if it does not at least purport to give to the person upon whom it is imposed a benefit equivalent to the amount paid. In other words, he believed that the doctrine promulgated in Norwood v. Baker should always hold. The exact difference between this doctrine and that of the court needs to be noted. The court looked only to the neighborhood upon which the assessment had been made, and tried to make sure that the assessment would not be greater than the benefits to be derived by that section as a section. Justice Harlan wished to look deeper and ascertain whether the individuals who had to pay the money would stand a reasonable chance of getting value received. The illogicality of the court's decree is evident. Under such law it is possible that some will pay for benefits enjoyed only by others. That, however, is the law, and it seems to have been established because of ease of application.[6]

In concluding this review of Justice Harlan's opinions regarding due process of law, it is seen that he was violently opposed to any alteration of the time-honored jury system; that he believed that public office should be considered property, of which one could not be deprived without due process of law; and that in levying special assessments attempt should always be made to find out whether the individual is likely to be benefited to the amount of the assessment levied. On each of these points he differed from the court, and stood by these principles to the last.

---

[6] See also Wight v. Davidson, 181 U. S. 374, and Tonawanda v. Lyon, 181 U. S. 389, for similar dissents by Justice Harlan.

CHAPTER IV

INTERSTATE AND FOREIGN COMMERCE

Liquor Legislation.—The question of interstate and foreign commerce is probably the most involved one in constitutional law. Its difficulty is lessened in the present instance by reason of the fact that it will not be necessary to review it in all its aspects. On the questions here involved Justice Harlan held, in certain respects, as decided views as on any other subject. With reference to state liquor legislation there are two marked dissents, which, though they are now mainly of historic value, will be of interest in showing his insight into what was to come. The two cases are Bowman v. Chicago and Northwestern R. Co., 125 U. S. 465, and Rhodes v. Iowa, 170 U. S. 412.

In the former case there is called into question a statute of the State of Iowa which attempted to forbid the transportation of spirituous liquors into that State. The case came up in a suit for damages against the railroad company for refusing because of the Iowa law to accept a shipment of beer from Chicago consigned to a place in Iowa. The court held, in accordance with the plea of the liquor dealers, that the statute in question was unconstitutional, for the following reasons: First, it was a burden on interstate commerce in that it impeded the free interchange of goods between Illinois and Iowa. " In the present case, the defendant is sued as a common carrier in the State of Illinois, and the breach of duty alleged against it is a violation of the law of that State in refusing to receive and transport goods which, as a common carrier, by that law, it was bound to accept and carry. It interposes as a defense a law of the State of Iowa, which forbids the delivery of such goods within that State. Has the law of Iowa any extraterritorial force which does not belong to the law of the State of Illinois? If the law of Iowa forbids the delivery, and the law of Illinois requires the transportation, which of the two shall prevail? How can the former make void the latter?" Second, the Constitution does not leave it to the States to say what shall or shall not be suitable articles of commerce. To hold otherwise would be to assert that "it has left to each State, according to its own caprice and arbitrary will, to discriminate for or against every article grown, produced, manufactured or sold in any State and sought to be introduced as an article of commerce into any other." Third, the Iowa law was not a legitimate exercise of the police power. "It is not one of those local regulations designed to aid and facilitate commerce; it is not an inspection law to secure the due quality and measure of a commodity; it is not a law to regulate or restrict the sale of an article deemed injurious to the health and morals of the community; it is not a regulation confined to the purely internal and domestic commerce of the State; it is not a restriction which only operates upon property after it has become mingled with and forms part of the mass of the property within the State. It is, on the other hand, a regulation directly affecting interstate commerce in an essential and vital point. . . . The right to prohibit sales, so far as conceded to the States, arises only after the act of transportation has terminated, because the sales which the State may forbid are of things within its jurisdiction."

The above outline gives the attitude of the court in this case. The following quotation will indicate the position which Justice Harlan assumed: "The fundamental question, therefore, is whether Iowa may lawfully restrict the bringing of intoxicating liquors from other States into her limits, by any person or carrier for another person or corporation, except such as are consigned to persons authorized by her laws to buy and sell them for the special purposes indicated. In considering this question, we are not left to conjecture as to the motives prompting the enactment of these statutes; for it is conceded that the prohibition upon common carriers bringing intoxicating liquors from other States, except under the foregoing conditions, was adopted as subservient to the general design of protecting the health and morals and the peace and good order of the people of Iowa against the physical and moral evils resulting from the unrestricted manufacture or sale of intoxicating liquors."

Justice Harlan's argument rests upon the assertion that liquors are inherently not suitable articles of commerce. " It is admitted that a State may prevent the introduction, within her limits, of rags or other goods infected with disease, or of cattle or meat or other provisions which, from their condition, are unfit for human use or consumption ; because, it is said, such articles are not merchantable or legitimate subjects of trade and commerce. But suppose the people of a State believe, upon reasonable grounds, that the general use of intoxicating liquors is dangerous to the public peace, the public health and the public morals; what authority has Congress or the judiciary to review their judgment upon that subject, and compel them to submit to a condition of things which they regard as destructive of their happiness and the peace and good order of society? If, consistently with the Constitution of the United States, a State can protect her sound cattle . . . she ought not to be deemed disloyal to that Constitution when she seeks by similar legislation to protect her people and their homes against the introduction of articles which are, in good faith, and not unreasonably, regarded by her citizens as 'laden with infection' more dangerous to the public than diseased cattle, or than rags containing the germs of disease."

The next argument presented by Justice Harlan was that the framers of the Constitution could not have intended— whether Congress had or had not chosen to act upon this subject—" to withhold from a State authority to prevent the introduction into her midst of articles or commodities, the manufacture of which, within her limits, she could prohibit, without impairing the constitutional rights of her own people. . . . Even the constitutional prohibition upon laws impairing the obligation of contracts does not restrict the power of the State to protect the health, the morals, or the safety of the community, as the one or the other may be involved in the execution of such contracts." In further substantiation of the contention that the police power of the State allowed the State to regulate almost anything that had to do with public health and morals he cited the case of Wilson v. Blackbird Creek Marsh Co., 2 Pet. 245. Other cases are cited which bear on this point. " The reserved power of the States to guard the health, morals and safety of their people is more vital to the existence of society than their power in respect to trade and commerce having no possible connection with those subjects."

It is difficult to overemphasize the importance of the case of Bowman v. Chicago and Northwestern R. Co. in its relation to the bearing of liquor legislation of the States upon interstate commerce. This was the first time that such legislation was contested before the Supreme Court. Here, as Justice Harlan showed, the court had plenty of authority to declare such legislation constitutional. As a matter of fact, the court had to go out of its way to declare the law unconstitutional. Here once and for all the relation between liquor legislation and interstate commerce could have been settled by declaring spirituous liquors unfit articles of commerce, of such a kind as ought not to be forced upon the States against their wills. If the decision, therefore, had been made according to Justice Harlan's doctrine, the whole history of this matter would have been changed. There would have been no need for the Wilson Bill, or for the Webb-Kenyon Act which puts into the hands of the States exactly the power that an affirmative decision in this case would have done. The tangle which has resulted would have been avoided.[1]

To follow out the progress of the doctrine of the Supreme Court relating to the traffic in intoxicating liquors the case of In re Rahrer, 140 U. S. 545, must next be con-

---

[1] Note the case of Leisy v. Hardin, 135 U. S. 100, where Justice Harlan concurred in a dissent upon similar grounds.

sidered. This case involved the constitutionality of a statute of Congress which tried to undo the mischief done by
the Bowman case. This act, known as the Wilson Act, provided that "upon arrival" of the liquor in any State or territory it should become subject to the laws there. This law
was declared constitutional, and seemed to be the remedy for
the situation. Justice Harlan dissented from the reasoning
of the court, but agreed with the decree. Since no opinion
is stated by him it cannot be known upon what ground he
differed from the court. It is sufficient to say that in this
case a law was declared constitutional which seemed to give
the States full power to control the liquor traffic, and that
Mr. Harlan agreed that it was constitutional.

When, however, a case came up under the Wilson Act, the
interpretation which the court gave to the phrase "upon
arrival in a State" overthrew the force of the act. In this
case, though Justice Harlan did not submit a separate dissenting opinion, he concurred in one given by Justice Gray.[2]
This case, Rhodes v. Iowa, 170 U. S. 412, arose because
of the fact that an officer of the State of Iowa, acting under
authority of a state law, had seized and destroyed at the
border of the State a shipment of liquor from Illinois.
The statute in question was almost identically the same as
the one which had been declared unconstitutional in the
Bowman case, and the main point to be decided was whether
the subsequent act of Congress had made it constitutional
for States to pass laws like the one in question. Had Congress acted so as to remove the barrier of interstate commerce from the States in their attempts to pass laws forbidding the sale of liquor within their borders?

The court held that the statute of the State of Iowa was
constitutional, but in order to do so found it necessary so to
interpret the Wilson Act that laws passed by the States
under its operation were ineffective in driving out the liquor
business. The Wilson Act had stipulated that liquor should

---

[2] It must be noted that the case of O'Neil v. Vermont, 144 U. S.
323, would have involved this same point had the court taken jurisdiction. In that case Justice Harlan delivered a stinging dissent
because of the refusal of the court to determine the case.

become subject to state law "upon arrival in a State," but the court so interpreted this phrase that the goods could proceed to their destination without interruption. "Only after their coming into the State and the consummation of their shipment" did the goods become subject to the laws of the State. "The words 'shall upon arrival in such state or territory be subject to the operation and effect of the laws of such state or territory' in one sense might be held to mean arrival at the state line. But to so interpret them would necessitate isolating these words from the entire context of the act, and would compel a construction destructive of other provisions contained therein. But this would violate the fundamental rule requiring that a law be construed as a whole, and not by distorting or magnifying a particular word found in it. It is clearly contemplated that the word 'arrival' signified that the goods should actually come into the State, since it is provided that 'all fermented, distilled, or other intoxicating liquors or liquids transported into a state or territory,' and this is further accentuated by the other provision, 'or remaining therein for use, consumption, sale, or storage therein.'"

"This language makes it impossible in reason to hold that the law intended that the word 'arrival' should mean at the state line, since it presupposes the coming of the goods into the state for 'use, consumption, sale, or storage.'"

It is easy to see the nature of the argument. By indulging in the use of the "subtle signification of words and the niceties of verbal distinction" which they condemn as not furnishing a safe guide, the judges came to their conclusion. But it must be added that this was done under the assumption by the court that unless such a meaning were attached to the word "arrival" the act would not have been constitutional.

Naturally the dissenting opinion centered its argument in the word "arrival." It contended that no such distorted meaning needed to be attached to that word in order to

allow the Wilson Act to stand. It asserted and reinforced
the assertion that liquor legislation was a legitimate subject
for the police power of the State. That being true, there
was little question that the act of Congress was constitutional under the broader interpretation of the word "arrival," which was quoted as follows from Chief Justice
Marshall: "'To arrive' is a neuter verb, which when applied to an object moving from place to place designates the
fact of 'coming to' or 'reaching' one place from another,
or coming to or reaching a place by travelling or moving
towards it. If the place be designated, then the object which
reaches a place has arrived at it. A person who is coming
to Richmond has arrived when he enters the city. But it is
not necessary to the correctness of this term, that the place
at which the traveller arrives should be his ultimate destination, or the end of his journey. A person going from Richmond to Norfolk by water arrives within Hampton Roads
when he reaches that place; or if he diverges from that
direct course he arrives in Petersburg when he enters that
town. That is, I believe, the universal understanding of
the term."[3]

As is of course known, there has been another act of
Congress which in its meaning amounts to making it unlawful for any fermented liquors to be carried into any place
where the people have voted it out. The violations of this
act the States are left to punish as violations of their laws.
It seems to be generally accepted that this act will be declared constitutional. The situation is now just about as it
would have been had the Bowman case been decided according to Justice Harlan's doctrine. Spirituous liquors have
practically been declared an article that a State, if it pleases
to do so, may designate as unfit to be carried within its
borders.

Race.—Justice Harlan's attitude regarding legislation as
to race distinctions in interstate commerce may readily be
guessed. The question seems to have come up only as re-

---

[3] The Patriot, 1 Brock. 407.

gards the Jim Crow laws. There are two cases which are strongly in opposition to each other. In the one, Hall v. Decuir, 95 U. S. 485, the Supreme Court declared unconstitutional a statute of Louisiana which forbade the separation of races on steamboats, as being a burden placed by a State upon interstate commerce; and in the other, Louisville, N. O. and T. R. Co. v. Mississippi, 133 U. S. 587, it declared valid a law of Mississippi which required that the races be separated on the trains as not being a burden imposed by the State upon interstate commerce. A full discussion of the latter case will be sufficient to give the import of both. From the first decision Justice Harlan did not dissent, but from the other he did. The case came by writ of error to the Supreme Court of Mississippi to pass upon the constitutionality of a statute of that State which required separate coaches for colored people. The railroad company violated that law in refusing to furnish separate accommodations, and argued that the statute was unconstitutional in that it amounted to a regulation of interstate commerce.

In rendering the decision, the court, speaking through Justice Brewer, asserted that the statute affected commerce only within the State, and was therefore within the power of the State to pass. The main contention between Justice Harlan and the court was as to the precedent set by Hall v. Decuir. Justice Brewer attempted to explain away that case as follows: " So the decision was by its terms carefully limited to those cases in which the law practically interfered with interstate commerce. Obviously whether interstate passengers of one race should, in any portion of their journey, be compelled to share their cabin accommodation with colored passengers, was a question of interstate commerce, and to be determined by Congress alone. In this case the supreme court of Mississippi held that the statute applied solely to commerce within the State; and that construction, being the construction of the Statute of the State by the highest court, must be conclusive here. If it be a matter respecting wholly commerce within the State, and not interfering with commerce between the States, then obviously there is no violation of the commerce clause of the Federal Constitution." The two cases seem to admit tacitly that the Supreme Court of the United States will hold statutes discriminating against colored persons constitutional if the state courts will uphold them, but they do not seem to say that the court will declare statutes of the same nature unconstitutional if declared unconstitutional by the state courts.

This doctrine did not meet with Justice Harlan's approval. Commenting on the differentiation made by the court, he said: " In its application to passengers on vessels engaged in interstate commerce, the Louisiana enactment forbade the separation of the white and black races while such vessels were within the limits of that State. The Mississippi statute, in its application to passengers on railroad trains employed in interstate commerce, requires such separation of races, while the trains are within that State. I am unable to perceive how the former is a regulation of interstate commerce and the latter is not. It is difficult to understand how a State enactment requiring the separation of the white and black races on interstate carriers of passengers, is a regulation of commerce among the States, while a similar enactment forbidding such separation is not a regulation of that character." In other words, Justice Harlan said that the ruling of the state courts on the matter did not have weight. It was for the United States Supreme Court to say, and if they had said that one thing was interstate commerce, that thing was interstate commerce, even if the state court said that it was not.

This gives in sufficient fulness the nature of the above decisions and dissent. These seem to be the only cases in which there were decisions by the Supreme Court on the question of separation of races on interstate carriers. The dissent from Louisville, N. O. and T. R. Co. v. Mississippi seems to be the only assertion made by Justice Harlan regarding the bearing of such laws upon interstate commerce, but it can be readily seen that if he had had his way the Jim Crow laws would have been brushed aside.

The Sherman Anti-Trust Law.—In this subject are found Justice Harlan's most vigorous dissents. It was due to the fact that these cases were so much in the public eye that Justice Harlan became so prominently known as a dissenter. Though it is true that he gave more dissenting opinions in the earlier part of his life than he did in the later, yet his earlier dissents seem not to have attracted so much attention, probably because the subjects were less conspicuous. It may be asserted, therefore, that from the E. C. Knight case to his death Justice Harlan was more prominently before the public than at any previous time, and deservedly so, because his dissents were greater and rang more truly of the democratic spirit.

The first case arising under the anti-trust act of 1890 was that of United States v. E. C. Knight Co., 156 U. S. 1. Though this case is hardly any longer citable for precedent, it will be interesting to follow out the change of opinion on this subject on the part of the Supreme Court. The case came into the Supreme Court under the following circumstances: A corporation, chartered under the laws of Pennsylvania, had been arraigned before the United States circuit court of appeals for the third circuit for having violated the act of 1890, in that it had resorted to an unlawful restraint of trade in violation of the statute of the United States forbidding all monopoly in restraint of trade. The suit, therefore, was against the various companies which had conspired to form the American Sugar Refining Company. The circuit court of appeals decided in favor of the corporation, and the Supreme Court affirmed its decision.

The following is a synopsis of the decision of the Supreme Court: First, referring to a definition of the word "monopoly" mentioned by the counsel for the United States as being applicable in English law, the following comment was made: "But the monopoly and restraint denounced by the act are the monopoly and restraint of interstate and international trade or commerce, while the conclusion to be assumed on this record is that the result of the transaction complained of was the creation of a monopoly in the manufacture of a necessary of life.

"In the view which we take of the case, we need not discuss whether because the tentacles which drew the outlying refineries into the dominant corporation were separately put out, therefore there was no combination to monopolize; or, because, according to political economists, aggregations of capital may reduce prices, therefore the objection to concentration of power is relieved; or, because others were theoretically left free to go into the business of refining sugar, and the original stockholders of the Philadelphia refineries after becoming stockholders of the American Company might go into competition with themselves, or, parting with that stock, might set up again for themselves, therefore no objectionable restraint was imposed."

Second, the control of this matter was to be exercised by the States: "It is vital that the independence of the commercial power and of the police power, and the delimitation between them, however sometimes perplexing, should always be recognized and observed, for while the one furnishes the strongest bond of union, the other is essential to the preservation of the autonomy of the states as required by our dual form of government; and acknowledged evils, however grave and urgent they may appear to be, had better be borne, than the risk be run, in the effort to suppress them, of more serious consequences by resort to expedients of even doubtful constitutionality.

"It will be perceived how far reaching the proposition is that the power of dealing with a monopoly directly may be exercised by the general government whenever interstate or international commerce may be ultimately affected." Again: "It is true that the bill alleged that the products of these refineries were sold and distributed among the several states, and that all the companies were engaged in trade or commerce with the several states and with foreign nations; but this was no more than to say that trade and commerce served manufacture to fulfill its function."

Thus the argument of the court was placed expressly on two grounds, in the first place, that theoretically there was not a monopoly. Even though the syndicate did embrace all the sugar-refining companies in the country, that was no reason why others might not develop in the future. In the second place, in order to preserve the police power of the States it was advisable to leave such matters in their hands.

Justice Harlan's dissent may be quoted at length. "If it be true that a *combination* of corporations or individuals may, so far as the power of Congress is concerned, subject interstate trade, in any of its stages, to unlawful restraints, the conclusion is inevitable that the Constitution has failed to accomplish one primary object of the Union, which was to place commerce *among the states* under the control of the common government of all the people, and thereby relieve or protect it against burdens or restrictions imposed, by whatever authority, for the benefit of particular localities or special interests."

In answer to the question as to what is an unlawful restraint of trade he said: "A general restraint of trade has often resulted from *combinations* formed for the purpose of controlling prices by destroying the opportunity of buyers and sellers to deal with each other upon the basis of fair, open, free competition. Combinations of this character have frequently been the subject of judicial scrutiny, and have always been condemned as illegal because of their necessary tendency to restrain trade. Such combinations are against common right and are crimes against the public."

In reference to the inapplicability of the state power to this question he spoke as follows: "There is a trade among the several states which is distinct from that carried on within the territorial limits of a state. The regulation and control of the former is committed by the national Constitution to Congress. Commerce among the states, as this court has declared, is a unit, and in respect of that commerce this is one country, and we are one people. It may be regulated by rules applicable to every part of the United States, and state lines and state jurisdiction cannot interfere with the enforcement of such rules. The jurisdiction of the general government extends over every foot of territory within the United States. Under the power with which it is invested, Congress may remove unlawful obstructions, of whatever kind, to the free course of trade among the states. In so doing it would not interfere with the 'autonomy of the States,' because the power thus to protect interstate commerce is expressly given by the people of all the states. Interstate intercourse, trade, and traffic is absolutely free, except as such intercourse may be incidentally or indirectly affected by the exercise by the state of their reserved police powers."

A further comment upon the inconsistency of the view of the court is expressed in these words: "Undue restrictions or burdens upon the purchasing of goods, in the market for sale, to be transported to other states, cannot be imposed even by a state without violating the freedom of commercial intercourse guaranteed by the Constitution. But if a *state* within whose limits the business of refining sugar is exclusively carried on may not constitutionally impose burdens upon purchases of sugar *to be transported to other states,* how comes it that combinations of corporations or individuals, within the same state, may not be prevented by the national government from putting unlawful restraints upon the purchasing of that article *to be carried from the state in which such purchases are made?* If the national power is competent to repress *state* action in restraint of interstate trade as it may be involved in purchases of refined sugar to be transported from one state to another state, surely it ought to be deemed sufficient to prevent unlawful restraints attempted to be imposed by combinations of corporations or individuals upon those identical purchases; otherwise, illegal combinations of corporations or individuals may—so far as national power and interstate commerce are concerned—do, with impunity, what no state can do."

Thus it is seen that, according to Justice Harlan's interpretation of the opinion of the court, the court had declared to be within the jurisdiction of the State that which, by this decision, had more power than the States themselves had.

One other quotation will help to substantiate the doctrine set forth by Justice Harlan. He said: "After the fullest consideration I have been able to bestow upon this important question, I find it impossible to refuse my assent to this proposition: Whatever a state may do to protect its completely interior traffic or trade against unlawful restraints, the general government is empowered to do for the protection of the people of all the states—for this purpose one people—against unlawful restraints imposed upon interstate traffic or trade in articles that are to enter into commerce among the several states. If, as already shown, a state may prevent or suppress a *combination*, the effect of which is to subject its domestic trade to the restraints necessarily arising from their obtaining the absolute control of the sale of a particular article in general use by the community, there ought to be no hesitation in allowing to Congress the right to suppress a similar *combination* that imposes a like unlawful restraint upon interstate trade and traffic in that article. While the states retain, because they have never surrendered, full control of their complete internal traffic, it was not intended by the framers of the Constitution that any part of interstate commerce should be excluded from the control of Congress."

His doctrine might be summarized by saying that since the States were not allowed any control over interstate commerce, and since the regulation of corporations in their interstate relations constituted regulation of interstate commerce, or rather of a part of interstate commerce, the power expressly belonged to the national government. As will be seen, this later through the effort of Justice Harlan became the doctrine of the court. By that time much mischief had been done, and the court had lost the opportunity of cutting at the root of the growing evil.

In the case just discussed, Justice Harlan stood alone against the other members of the court. The next time he is found taking an active part in a decision on this point is in the case of the Northern Securities Co. v. United States, 193 U. S. 197. In several cases prior to that, however, the question had come up, but in not quite so aggravated a form. From only one of those cases did Justice Harlan dissent, and then with no opinion stated.[4]

In the case of the Northern Securities Co. v. United States Justice Harlan asserted, mainly in an affirmative way, the principles which he had developed in his dissent from the E. C. Knight case. The discussion is somewhat long, but much of the space is taken up in answering some of the arguments presented by the attorneys for the corporation, which answers are of no especial concern here. Quotations from this opinion will show how it served to overthrow the condemnable doctrine promulgated in the E. C. Knight case.

The Northern Securities case was very similar to the E. C. Knight case, the main difference being that the monopolization was of railroads instead of sugar. The suit, therefore, was against several railroad companies which had arranged to put a stop to competition in the north and northwestern sections of the United States by controlling under one head practically all of the railroads in the north and northwestern part of the United States. The question to be determined was whether such a combination amounted to a restraint of trade forbidden by the act of 1890, and whether the United States had the power to command these corporations to refrain from their proposed combination. The decision had been rendered against the Northern Se-

---

[4] U. S. v. Trans-Missouri Freight Assoc., 166 U. S. 290; U. S. v. Joint Traffic Assoc., 171 U. S. 505; Hopkins v. U. S., 171 U. S. 578; Addyston Pipe and Steel Co. v. U. S., 175 U. S. 211; Montague and Company v. Lowry, 193 U. S. 38; Anderson v. U. S., 171 U. S. 604 (combination legal, Justice Harlan dissented).

curities Company in the circuit court of the United States for the district of Minnesota, and this decision was affirmed by the Supreme Court, speaking through Justice Harlan.

The following quotation gives the general import of the majority opinion: "The mere existence of such a combination, and the power acquired by the holding company as its trustee, constitute a menace to, and a restraint upon, that freedom of commerce which Congress intended to recognize and protect, and which the public is entitled to have protected. If such combination be not destroyed, all the advantages that would naturally come to the public under operation of the general laws of competition, as between the Great Northern and Northern Pacific Railway Companies, will be lost, and the entire commerce of the immense territory in the northern part of the United States between the Great Lakes and the Pacific at Puget sound will be at the mercy of a single holding corporation, organized in a State distant from the people of that territory."

In answer to the contention that an affirmative decree in this case would make *ownership* of stock in a state railroad corporation a matter of interstate commerce, if that railroad were engaged in interstate traffic, the following reply is given: "Such statements as to issues in this case are, we think, wholly unwarranted, and are very wide of the mark; it is setting up mere men of straw to be easily stricken down. We do not understand that the government makes· any such contentions or takes any such positions as those statements imply. It does not contend that Congress may control the mere acquisition or the mere ownership of stock in a State corporation engaged in interstate commerce. Nor does it contend that Congress can control the organization of state corporations authorized by their charters to engage in interstate and international commerce. But it does contend that Congress may protect the freedom of interstate commerce by any means that are appropriate and that are lawful, and not prohibited by the Constitution. It does contend that no state corporation can stand in the way of the enforcement of the national will, legally expressed."

Another very telling blow at the contention that this doctrine would be a detriment to state autonomy is this: "If a state may strike down combinations that restrain its domestic commerce by destroying free competition among those engaged in such commerce, what power, except that of Congress, is competent to protect the freedom of interstate and international commerce when assailed by a combination that restrains such commerce by stifling competition among those engaged in it? . . . The argument in behalf of the defendants necessarily leads to such results, and places Congress, although invested by the people of the United States with full authority to regulate interstate and international commerce, in a condition of helplessness, so far as the protection of the public against such combination is concerned."

As is seen, even by the few quotations given, the decision in this case was a great one. Its arguments were convincing, its spirit showed a largeness of soul not often found among judges, and it sets a precedent that needed to be set much earlier. From that time on, therefore, the monstrous, soulless corporations have had over them the strongest power that this government affords. And, as has been seen, our thanks are largely due Justice Harlan for this evidently correct interpretation of the Constitution, for any other would simply have said that our constitution contained a grave flaw. Of course the situation could have been met with a constitutional amendment, but only after much more mischief had been done.

The two cases which have caused so much comment of late do not bear upon the present subject. They are the cases of the Standard Oil Co. v. United States, 221 U. S. 1, and the United States v. American Tobacco Co., 221 U. S. 106. Although Justice Harlan concurred in the conclusions arrived at in these cases, he dissented from the action of the court in reading the word "unreasonable" into the

Act of 1890. With him that was judicial legislation. These cases will, therefore, be discussed under that topic.[5]

From the cases given it seems possible to gain a sufficiently clear conception of Justice Harlan's doctrine concerning the so-called Sherman Anti-Trust Act. Though the court has not in all respects accepted his interpretation, it has practically done so. The weight of his influence on this point has probably been more significant than upon any other burning question. Amidst the wild political discussions he did not lose his balance, but always held closely to the interpretation of both the Constitution and an act of Congress, and on this subject, at least, demonstrated that the wisest thing for the court to do is to interpret and apply laws, not to change them. If Justice Harlan's doctrine had from the first predominated, the so-called twilight zone would have been much less in evidence.

Taxation.—According to the recognized law, any owner, whether individual or State, may impose a charge for the use of a wharf. This charge, however, cannot be too high, and must be levied with a view to keeping up the wharf, otherwise it becomes a burden upon interstate commerce and hence unconstitutional. This distinction sometimes gives rise to very fine differentiations in order to ascertain what is simply a wharfage charge, and what amounts to a duty of tonnage or poundage.

There seems to be only one case in which Justice Harlan was at variance with the court on this question. This was the case of Parkersburg and Ohio River Transportation Co. v. Parkersburg, 107 U. S. 691. The city of Parkersburg, West Virginia, levied under the guise of wharfage a tax upon vessels according to their capacity and the quantities of freight loaded or unloaded. The Parkersburg and Ohio River Transportation Company entered suit in the circuit court of the United States for that district, on the plea that the levy amounted to a duty of tonnage and that it was a restriction upon interstate commerce. The circuit

[5] Pages 199–202.

court held that the levy was a wharfage charge. The Supreme Court affirmed the decision, reinforcing the decree with complicated reasoning.

The core of the decision is found in the following quotation: "Now wharves, levees and landing places are essential to commerce by water, no less than a navigable channel and a clear river. But they are attached to the land; they are private property, real estate; and they are primarily, at least, subject to the local state laws. Congress has never yet interfered to supervise their administration; it has hitherto left this exclusively to the States. There is little doubt, however, that Congress, if it saw fit, in case of prevailing abuses in management of wharf property, . . . might interpose and make regulations to prevent such abuses. When it shall have done so, it will be time enough for the courts to put its regulations into effect by judicial proceedings properly instituted. But until Congress has acted, the courts of the United States cannot assume jurisdiction over the subject as a matter of Federal cognizance. It is the Congress, not the judicial department, to which the constitution has given power to regulate commerce with foreign nations and among the States. The courts can never take initiative on this subject."

From this it is seen that the court asserted that it was unwilling to take cognizance of a case of this kind in the absence of a statute of Congress. But it intimated further on that if the charge were extortionate it might take jurisdiction, but that ordinarily such things are in charge of the State unless Congress has acted on the subject.

Justice Harlan disagreed with this reasoning. With him the Constitution was express in forbidding tonnage and poundage, and he thought that it was for the court to decide whether or not any charge made by any state agency amounted to tonnage or poundage, or whether it was simply wharfage. In this case he contended that the levy was a duty of tonnage, and hence was unconstitutional. "It is conceded by the demurrer to the bill that, from these fees,

the City has long since been re-imbursed for the actual cost
of constructing the wharf; that the amount, annually collected for its use by boats, is largely in excess of any expense incurred in its maintenance and repair; that the
wharf has been permitted to become and remain in bad
repair, at times almost unfit for use; that nearly all the
money so raised is applied by the City to increase its general
revenue, and to payment of its indebtedness; lastly, that
the wharfage charges are *unreasonable in amount and
oppressive.* . . .

"In the opinion of the court, a duty of tonnage is defined to be a charge, tax or duty on a vessel for the mere
privilege of entering or lying in a port. The City of Parkersburg cannot, therefore, constitutionally impose a charge,
tax or duty upon or for the exercise of that privilege. Now,
do the Constitution and the existing laws of the United
States extend their protection no further than to secure the
bare, naked right of entering a port free from local burdens
or duties upon its exercise? May not the boat, in virtue
of the Constitution and existing laws, also land at any
wharf, at least at any public wharf, on the Ohio River for
the purpose of discharging and receiving freight and passengers? Of what value would be the right to enter the
port without the privilege of landing its passengers and
freight? Is not the substantial privilege of landing passengers and freight necessarily involved in the right of
entering the port? If so, it would seem that the right to
land a boat at a public wharf on a navigable water of the
United States, is as fully protected by the Constitution and
the existing laws of the United States, as of entering the
port. A charge, tax or duty imposed upon the exercise of
the right to land is, consequently, for every practical purpose, as much a duty of tonnage as a charge, tax or duty
upon the privilege of entering the port."

His conclusion is as follows: "The opinion of the court,
I repeat, rests necessarily upon the ground that the enforced exaction and collection by a municipal corporation

of unreasonable compensation for the use of its wharf by a boat, duly enrolled and licensed under the laws of the United States, and engaged in commerce upon the Ohio River, does not infringe or impair any right given or secured either by the Constitution or the existing laws of the United States. To that proposition I am unable to give my assent."

It is plain, therefore, that Justice Harlan could not see how a levy could be a wharfage charge when none of the proceeds were applied to the up-keep of the wharf, or how it could fail to be a tonnage charge when the rate was specified at so much a ton. Nor could he see how the court could refuse to pass upon the constitutionality of an action when that action clearly involved the interpretation of a clause of the Constitution. To summarize his doctrine on this matter, it might be said that he believed that it was within the jurisdiction of the court, regardless of the fact that Congress had not acted, to decide in any case whether a fee charged for the use of a wharf amounted to a duty of tonnage or poundage or a restriction upon interstate commerce, or whether it was simply a levy to cover the expense of the construction and repair of the wharf.

In the case of Ficklen v. Shelby County Taxing District, 145 U. S. 1, is found a very interesting dissent on the part of Justice Harlan, in which he accused the court of allowing discrimination in taxation, and discrimination of a kind that amounted to a burden on interstate commerce. An out-of-the-State concern had representatives in Shelby County, Tennessee. These representatives were simply agents, having a definite location for the exhibition of their wares and for taking orders of goods to be shipped into the State. In addition to a license fee of fifty dollars, the State, or rather the county, undertook to levy a tax of two and a half per cent on the profits made by one of these representatives. The plaintiff set up the plea that such a tax by the State amounted to a burden upon interstate commerce. The court held that this was not such a burden, but that a State has power to tax all property having a situs within its limits whether it is employed in interstate commerce or not.

"No doubt can be entered of the right of a state Legislature to tax trades, professions, and occupations, in the absence of inhibition in the state constitution in that regard, and where a resident citizen engages in general business subject to a particular tax, the fact that the business done chances to consist, for the time being, wholly or partially in negotiating sales between resident and non-resident merchants of goods situated in another State does not necessarily involve the taxation of interstate commerce, forbidden by the Constitution."

Justice Harlan dissented from this ruling. At the outset he said: "It seems to me that the opinion and judgment in this case are not in harmony with the numerous decisions of this court. I do not assume that the court intends to modify or overrule any of those cases, because no such purpose is expressed. And yet I feel sure that the present decision will be cited as having that effect."

He said further: "The principles announced in these cases, if fairly applied to the present case, ought, in my judgment, to have led to a conclusion different from that reached by the court. Ficklen took out a license as merchandise broker and gave bond to make a return of the gross commissions earned by him. His commissions in 1887 were wholly derived from interstate business, that is, from mere orders taken in Tennessee for goods in other states, to be shipped into that State, when the orders were forwarded and filled. He was denied a license for 1888 unless he first paid two and a half per cent on his gross commissions. And the court holds that it was consistent with the Constitution of the United States for the local authorities of the taxing district of Shelby County to make it a condition precedent to Ficklen's right to a license for 1888 that he should pay the required per cent of the gross commissions earned by him in 1887 in interstate business. This is a very clever device to enable the taxing district of Shelby County to sustain its government by taxation upon interstate commerce."

The following distinctions are drawn in conclusion: " The result of the present decision is, that while under *Robbins* v. *Shelby County Tax. Dist.,* a license tax may not be imposed in Tennessee upon drummers for soliciting there the sale of goods to be brought from other states; while under *Leloup v. Port of Mobile,* a local license tax cannot be imposed in respect to telegrams between points in different states; and while under *Stoutenburgh* v. *Hennick,* commercial agents cannot be taxed in the District of Columbia for soliciting there the sale of goods to be brought into the District from one of the states; the taxing district of Shelby County may require, as a condition of granting a license as merchandise broker, that the applicant shall pay a license fee, and, in addition 2½ per cent upon the gross commissions received, not only in the business transacted by him that is wholly domestic, but in that which is wholly interstate."

The last quotations show clearly the ground of Justice Harlan's dissent. He could see no reason for refusing at one time to allow the State to tax persons in one category, and at a later date allowing it to tax another person in a similar situation. It must be admitted, however, that the situations were only apparently similar. The dissent was due to the fact that the tax was in effect upon interstate trade, and only interstate trade, for proof was present that the agent in question had done no intrastate business. With the court the fact that the man did only interstate business was immaterial, since his license granted him the right to sell goods produced within the State. Justice Harlan contended, however, that since the man in fact did no intrastate business he was beyond the taxing power of the State.

The question of state taxation of federal franchises is a complex one. It appears, however, that the Supreme Court has done much to complicate instead of simplify the situation. The case of the Central Pacific R. Co. v. California, 162 U. S. 91, will bear out this assertion. This case came to the Supreme Court by writ of error from the supreme court of California. According to the railroad company's estimate, its taxable property in the State of California amounted to $12,273,785, while according to the estimate of the Board of Equalization the amount was $18,000,000. The railroad company objected because the Board of Equalization had included within its assessment the value of the company's federal franchise to engage in the business of interstate commerce, and said that this was unconstitutional in that it was a burden laid by the State upon a federal agency. The court decided against the railroad company upon the following grounds: The rights and privileges of doing business have value as taxable property, and in addition to the federal franchise there was a state franchise, admitted by the company. Upon this admitted franchise the State could place a tax. Since the express valuation of the state franchise was not given, the extra assessment could be taken to mean a tax by the State upon the state franchise.

Justice Harlan did not agree with this line of argument. He felt that if the State were allowed to tax as highly as it pleased the state franchise of a federal agency, that power might enable the State in certain instances seriously to hamper the performance of federal functions. He said: "If the assessment in question had been separately upon the visible property of the company, as distinguished from its franchises, the case would have presented a different aspect; and we should then have been compelled to re-examine the question as to the extent to which the property of the company, used in accomplishing the objects designed by Congress, could be taxed by the State. But, as the opinion of the court shows, the present assessment was upon the franchise, railway, roadbed, rails, and rolling stock of the company without stating separately their respective values. That which was invalid cannot be separated from that which was valid. So that the question is presented whether it is competent for the State to sell for its taxes the franchise of the company. If it cannot the whole assessment is void.

"I cannot agree that the franchise which the corporation has received from the United States and the state can be assessed by the state for taxation along with its roadbed, right of way, etc., and then sold. That is taxation of one of the instrumentalities of the national government, which no state may do without the consent of the Congress of the United States. Of course, this corporation ought to contribute its due share to support the government of each state within whose limits its property is situated and its privileges exercised. But it is for Congress to prescribe the rule of taxation to be applied at least to the franchises of the corporation, which, although created by the state, is as much a federal agency as if it had been created a corporation by national enactment. It has never heretofore been recognized that a state could, without the assent of Congress, sell for its taxes the franchises, rights, and privileges employed, under the authority of the national government, to accomplish national objects, particularly when such franchises, rights, and privileges are under mortgage to secure the government specified liabilities."

Justice Harlan held that if there was a federal franchise and at the same time a state franchise, the State should not be allowed to tax the state franchise without a separate specification as to what was the rate and amount of the tax on the state franchise; and above all the State should not be allowed the power to hamper by taxation a federal instrumentality.

Justice Harlan has differed from the court in two interesting cases with reference to export taxes, in one case saying that what the court claimed was a tax upon exports was not one, and in the other case arguing that what the court asserted was not a tax on exports was one.

The first of these cases is that of Fairbank v. United States, 181 U. S. 283. Here was contested the stamp duty levied upon various forms of commercial paper to help defray the expenses of the Spanish-American War, as applied to bills of lading accompanying shipments to foreign ports. The plea was set up that a tax of ten cents on every such bill of lading amounted to a duty upon exports, forbidden by the Constitution in Article 1, Par. 9, which reads that "no tax or duty shall be laid on any article exported from any State."

The court with a majority of one declared that such a tax amounted to a duty on exports in that the bill of lading was an essential accompaniment of articles of commerce. "We are of opinion that a stamp tax on a foreign bill of lading is in substance and effect equivalent to a tax on the articles included in that bill of lading, and, therefore, a tax or duty on exports, and in conflict with the constitutional prohibition."

Justice Harlan, with whom concurred Justices Gray, White, and McKenna, opposed this view. The grounds upon which they rested their arguments were two. In the first place, they held that since it had been the practice of the nation since 1797 at intervals to impose such a stamp tax, it was too late now to challenge the constitutionality of it. In the second place, a simple tax of ten cents upon a bill of lading of a large shipment of goods could not in fact amount to a duty upon exports, but was a tax on the paper.

In support of the first contention the several instances in which such a tax had been levied and collected were cited, and the fact was urged that not before within the century had they been even questioned. It should be mentioned that the majority had not passed lightly over this point, as is shown by the following words: "It must be borne in mind also in respect to this matter that during the first period exports were limited, and the amount of the stamp duty was small, and that during the second period we were passing through the stress of a great civil war, or endeavoring to carry its enormous debt; so that it is not strange that the legislative action in this respect passed unchallenged. Indeed, it is only of late years, when the burdens of taxation are increasing by reason of the great expenses of government, that the objects and modes of taxation have become a matter of special scrutiny. But the delay in presenting these questions is no excuse for not giving them full consideration and determining them in accordance with the true meaning of the Constitution."

The other point, which seems to be the stronger, was not answered by the majority, though they alluded to it with the assertion that the power to tax is the power to destroy. The following quotation will show the reasoning of the minority in this regard: "It is said that the power to tax is the power to destroy, and that if Congress can impose a stamp tax of 10 cents upon the vellum, parchment, or paper on which is written a bill of lading for articles to be exported from a state, it could as well impose a duty of $5,000, and thereby indirectly tax the articles intended for export. That conclusion would by no means follow. A *stamp* duty has now, and has had for centuries, a well-defined meaning. It has always been distinguished from an ordinary tax measured by the value or kind of the property taxed. If Congress, in respect of a bill of lading for articles to be exported, had imposed a tax of $5,000 for and in respect of the vellum, parchment, or paper upon which such bill was written, the courts, looking beyond form and considering substance, might well have held that such an act was contrary to the settled theory of stamp-tax laws, and that the purpose and necessary operation of such legislation was, in violation of the Constitution, to tax the articles specified in such bill, and not to impose simply a stamp duty. Here, the small duty imposed, without reference to the kind, quantity, or value of the articles exported, renders it certain that when Congress imposed such duty specifically on the vellum, parchment, or paper upon which the bill of lading was written or printed, it meant what it so plainly said; and no ground exists to impute a purpose by indirection to tax the articles exported."

An interesting contrast to the Fairbank case is found in Cornell v. Coyne, 192 U. S. 418. Here the court upheld a statute which placed a direct tax of one per cent per pound on filled cheese. The contention was raised by Cornell, the manufacturer of the cheese, that this tax did not apply to that part of his products which was intended expressly for filling foreign orders. In spite of the decision in the Fairbank case, however, the court did not sustain his contention. No special argument was presented except that the cheese before shipment was just like other cheese which was intended for home consumption, and if part of it had to bear a tax all of it should. "The true construction of the constitutional provision," said the judge, "is that no burden by way of tax or duty be cast upon the exportation of articles, and does not mean that articles exported are relieved from prior ordinary burdens of taxation which rest upon all property similarly situated. The exemption attaches to the export, and not to the article before exportation."

Justice Harlan opposed the reasoning of the court on two grounds, in the first place, because of the possibility of great abuse developing from such a decree; and, in the second place, because it was inconsistent with the doctrine established in the Fairbank case, from which, it is to be noted, he dissented. Of the first point he said this: "The result would be that Congress, in time of peace, and by means of taxation, could bring about a condition of utter occlusion between the manufacturers of this country and the markets of other countries. Indeed, the several states could bring about that result by taxation; for if an article manufactured for exportation and which was prepared for exportation as soon as the manufacture was completed, is not an *export* from the moment such preparation was begun, then a state may impose a tax upon it as *property* and compel the payment thereof before the article is removed from its limits for exportation. I do not think that the framers of the Constitution contemplated such a condition as possible."

As regards the second point he made the following assertion: "In the *Fairbank case* the court held that a mere stamp tax on a bill of lading taken at the time articles were shipped from a state to a foreign country was a tax on the articles themselves as exports, and was forbidden by the constitutional provision that no tax or duty shall be laid on articles exported from any state. It is now held that a tax on articles admittedly manufactured only for exportation, and not for sale or consumption in this country, and which are exported as soon as they can be made ready for shipment, after the completion of manufacture, in execution of contracts entered into prior to the commencement of manufacture, is a tax on the articles themselves *as property,* and not on them as exports. . . . Thus, despite the express prohibition of all taxes or duties upon articles exported from the states, Congress is recognized as having the same power over exports from the several states as it has exercisd over imports from foreign countries. I do not think that it has such power."

It is interesting to note the contrast between Justice Harlan's dissent from this case and that from the Fairbank case. In the former his argument was that the tax in question could not properly be construed to be a tax upon exports, because it was so small that it was impossible that it should affect the price of the article exported. In this case he asserted that the tax could not be construed in any other way, since the tax of one cent a pound on the exported cheese necessarily raised the price that much. But he seemed not to recognize that the tax on the cheese was not placed there because of its exportation. If the tax were on the export because it was an export, it would come within the constitutional provision; otherwise it would not. Yet if the Constitution is to be interpreted to mean that the framers wished to encourage exportation by exempting exports from all taxation, Justice Harlan's doctrine in this case will have to be accepted as correct. Such an interpretation, however, seems to be a discrimination against the home consumer.

A very hotly contested case on the question of the ability of a State to tax the gross receipts[6] of a railroad doing part interstate and part intrastate commerce was that of Galveston, Harrisburg, and San Antonio R. Co. v. Texas, 210 U. S. 217. In this case was contested an attempt of the State of Texas to impose a tax "equal to one per cent of their gross receipts" upon railway companies whose lines lay wholly within the State. The company sought to have refunded money which it had paid under such a levy, on the plea that the tax constituted a burden on interstate commerce.

The argument of the court, speaking through Justice Holmes, is found in the following quotation: "We are of the opinion that the statute levying this tax does amount to an attempt to regulate commerce among the States. The distinction between a tax 'equal to' 1 per cent of gross receipts, and a tax of 1 per cent of the same seems to us nothing, except where the former phrase is the index of an actual attempt to reach the property and to let the interstate traffic and the receipts from it alone. We find no such attempt or anything to qualify the plain inference from the statute taken by itself. On the contrary, we rather infer from the judgment of the state court and from the argument on behalf of the state that another tax on the property of the railroad is upon a valuation of that property taken as a going concern. This is merely an effort to reach the gross receipts, not even disguised by the name of an occupation

---

[6] For a significant discussion of the importance of this subject, and how the court got itself out of the evil effects of this decision, see E. R. A. Seligman, Essays in Taxation, ch. viii, pp. 264–270.

tax, and in no way helped by the words 'equal to.'" As is seen, the contention centered around the wording of the statute, that the tax should be " equal to " the gross receipts. The court held that the State had attempted to make a distinction between a tax *equal to* and a tax *on* the gross receipts, in other words, that the gross receipts should be a gauge of the amount of business done in the State. This distinction was considered not well founded.

Justice Harlan, however, with whom concurred Justices Fuller, White, and McKenna, thought this a valid tax. Justice Harlan's reasons for not considering the tax an improper burden upon interstate commerce are mainly two. First, such a tax did constitute an occupation tax upon business within the State of Texas, which had been declared to be constitutional under the Texas constitution. " Such is the construction which the state court places on the statute, and that construction is justified by the words used. We have the authority of the Supreme Court of Texas for saying that the Constitution of that state authorizes the imposition of occupation taxes upon natural persons and upon corporations, other than municipal, doing business in that state. The plaintiff in error is a Texas corporation, and it cannot be doubted that the state may impose an occupation tax on one of its own corporations, provided such a tax does not interfere with the exercise of some power belonging to the United States."

Second, the minority held that the burden upon interstate commerce would be incidental and not direct, and hence would be constitutional, as the court had often previously asserted. " The state only measures the occupation tax by looking at the entire amount of the business done within its limits without reference to the source from which the business comes. It does not tax any part of the business because of its being interstate. It has reference equally to all kinds of business done by the corporation in the state. Suppose that the state, as, under its constitution it might do, should impose an income tax upon railroad corporations of its own creation, doing business within the state, equal to a given per cent of all incomes received by the corporation from its business,—would the corporation be entitled to have excluded from computation such of its income as was derived from interstate commerce? Such would be its right under the principles announced in the present case. In the case supposed the income tax would, under the principles or rules now announced, be regarded as a direct burden upon interstate commerce. I cannot assent to that view."

Justice Harlan's contention was, therefore, that the gauging of the amount of the tax by the gross receipts of a railroad company may have constituted an unsound method of taxation, yet since it could not be fairly said to be a direct burden upon interstate commerce, or opposed to any other prohibition in the United States Constitution, it was a valid method. This seems to be an instance when the liberality of the court allowed it to go into the merit of a state law and forbid it, even though there was not a really fair basis upon which to rest this disallowance.

Freedom of Contract.—The question of freedom of contract might well be discussed under a different heading, but since the specific cases so closely concern commerce, the matter may be taken up here. There are two cases in which the principle was primarily involved, namely, Hooper v. California, 155 U. S. 648, and Robertson v. Baldwin, 165 U. S. 275. The first involved a contract for insurance which was entered into contrary to the laws of California. The second involved the compulsion of seamen to perform their contracts.

The facts of the first case were these: Hooper was an agent for Johnson and Higgins, duly organized brokers in New York, who conducted an office in California according to the laws of that State. A citizen of California named Mott applied to Hooper to procure a certain amount of insurance for a vessel, named the *Alliance*. This Hooper succeeded in doing through his employers in the city of New York, who, in turn, secured the insurance from a Boston company which was not licensed to do business in California. The question was, could the California statute which forbade this transaction operate in this case, or was it an interference with privileges granted under the Constitution,— granted in the first place in the commerce clause, and in the second place in the fourteenth amendment. The court, speaking through Justice White, answered the question in the negative. Justice Harlan said that it should have been answered affirmatively.

The reasons for the holding of the court may be briefly stated as follows: First, insurance business had been declared not to be commerce, and the exclusive control by Congress of marine affairs did not alter this declaration. Insurance policies were no more articles of commerce on the sea than on the land. "The business of insurance is not commerce. The contract of insurance is not an instrumentality of commerce. The making of such a contract is a mere incident of commercial intercourse, and in this respect there is no difference whatever between insurance against fire and insurance against 'the perils of the sea.'" Second, Hooper could not be considered an agent of Mott in procuring this insurance for him, but he had to be looked upon as an agent of the Boston company, which was not licensed to do business in California, and hence Mott was not unconstitutionally deprived of his liberty of contract. "If the contention of the plaintiff in error were admitted, the established authority of the state to prevent a foreign corporation from carrying on business within its limits, either absolutely or except upon certain conditions, would be destroyed. It would be only necessary for such a corporation to have an understanding with a resident that in the effecting of contracts between itself and other residents of the state, he should be considered the agent of the insured persons, and not of the company. This would make the exercise of a substantial and valuable power by a state government depend not on the actual facts of the transactions over which it lawfully seeks to extend its control, but upon the disposition of a corporation to resort to a mere subterfuge in order to evade obligations properly imposed upon it. Public policy forbids a construction of the law which leads to such a result, unless logically unavoidable."

Justice Harlan dissented upon the following grounds: "We have before us a statute making it a crime to procure or agree to procure, in California, for a resident of that state, a policy of insurance from a foreign corporation which does not propose to do business there by agents, and, so far as appears, has never issued to a resident of California any policy but the one issued to Mott." This he goes on to say "is an illegal interference with the liberty both of Mott and of Hooper, as well as an abridgment of the privileges, not of a foreign corporation, but of individual citizens of other states through whom the policy in question was obtained."

He said further: "If he [Mott] preferred insurance in a company that had no agent in California, he had a right to that preference; and any interference with its free exercise would infringe his liberty. Suppose he had himself applied, by mail, directly to Johnson & Higgins for insurance on his vessel, and that firm had delivered the policy in question to an express company with directions to deliver it to Mott. Or, suppose that Mott had made his application, by mail, directly to the company. I cannot believe that a statute making his conduct, in either of the cases supposed, a criminal offence, would be sustained as consistent with the constitutional guaranties of liberty. But, it seems from the opinion of the court, that a state is at liberty to treat one as a criminal for doing for another that which the latter might himself do of right and without becoming a criminal. In my judgment a state cannot make it a crime for one of its people to obtain, himself or through the agency of individual citizens of another state, insurance upon his property by a foreign corporation that chooses not to enter the former state by its own agents."

This brings out clearly enough the ground of Justice Harlan's dissent. But when one considers the import of the reasoning here set forth one must admit that according to this doctrine an insurance company could do business within a State without complying with the laws of that State. In this case Justice Harlan doubtless let his fondness for freedom get the better of his judgment. If the above case had gone according to his doctrine, the declaration that insurance policies are not articles of commerce would have been useless, for, as the majority opinion pointed out, the insurance companies could do all business through representatives without of necessity complying with the state laws. Though there is no direct assertion to that effect, one feels from this decision that Justice Harlan thought that insurance policies ought to have been declared articles of commerce.

In Robertson v. Baldwin, 165 U. S. 275, Justice Harlan dissented more vigorously along lines similar to those of the Hooper case. The circumstances and argument of this case can be stated very briefly. Certain seamen were arrested in San Francisco and forced, against their will, to go back to work on a vessel engaged in commerce. The employers claimed that the men had agreed to work in this vessel until it should return to some port in the United States. The plea of the seamen was that the act of Congress authorizing their seizure by a justice of peace and return to the vessel was unconstitutional in that it forced them into involuntary servitude.

The majority of the court held that the contract of seamen differs from other contracts. Tracing the laws from the earliest times, Justice Brown, rendering the opinions of the court, showed that sailors have always had this coercion applied to them. "In the face of this legislation upon the subject of desertion and absence without leave, which was in force in this country for more than sixty years before the 13th Amendment was adopted, and similar legislation abroad from time immemorial, it cannot be open to doubt that the provision against involuntary servitude was never intended to apply to their contracts."

Justice Harlan looked at this question differently. He contended that such compulsion was involuntary servitude, and that citations from history had no bearing since, throughout history, slavery itself had been legal. Nor did he think that the nature of the undertaking gave sufficient reason to force the men to work. In regard to this last point he said: "Under the contract of service, it was at the volition of the master to entail service upon these appellants for an indefinite period. So far as the record discloses, it was an accident that the vessel came back to San Francisco when it did. By the shipping articles, the appellants could not quit the vessel until it returned to a port of the United States, and such return depended absolutely upon the will of the master. He had only to land at foreign ports, and keep the vessel away from the United States, in order to prevent the applicants from leaving his service."

In connection with the other consideration the following quotation is interesting: "The 13th Amendment, although tolerating involuntary servitude only when imposed as a punishment of crime of which the party shall have been duly convicted, has been construed, by the decision just rendered, as if it contained an additional clause expressly excepting from its operation seamen who engage to serve on private vessels. Under this view of the Constitution, we may now look for advertisements, not for runaway servants as in the days of slavery, but for runaway seamen. In former days, overseers could stand with whip in hand over slaves, and force them to perform personal service for their masters. While, with the assent of all, that condition of things has ceased to exist, we can but be reminded of the past when it is adjudged to be consistent with the law of the land for freemen who happen to be seamen to be held in custody that they may be forced to go aboard private vessels and render personal services against their will."

From the above it is seen that Justice Harlan did not believe that Congress, under its power over interstate and foreign commerce, could pass laws which would abridge the rights of seamen, any more legitimately that it could abridge the rights of any other class of workmen.

Along the same line with the case just discussed is the case of Geer v. Connecticut, 161 U. S. 519. In this case it was held that it is not unconstitutional for a State to forbid, under pain of fine or imprisonment, that its citizens ship game killed within the boundaries of the State to any point outside of the State. The ground for the decision was that a State may preserve the game for its own people. "The power of a state to protect by adequate police regulation its people against the adulteration of articles of food . . . although in doing so commerce might be remotely affected, necessarily carries with it the existence of a like power to preserve a food supply which belongs in common to all the people of the state, which can only become the subject of ownership in a qualified way, and which can never become the object of commerce except with the consent of the state and, subject to the conditions which it may deem best to impose for public good."

Justice Harlan dissented. He held that after a man has gained possession of killed game, it becomes his own, to deal with as he pleases. He said: "The game in question having been lawfully killed, the person who killed it and took it into his possession became the rightful owner thereof. This, I take it, will not be questioned. As such owner he could dispose of it by gift or sale, at his discretion. So long as it was fit for use as food, the state could not interfere with his disposition of it, any more than it could interfere with the disposition by the owner of other personal property that was not noxious in its character. To hold that the person receiving personal property from the owner may not receive it with the intent to send it out of the state is to recognize an arbitrary power in the government which is inconsistent with the liberty belonging to every man, as well as with the rights which inhere in the ownership of property. . . . Believing that the statute of Connecticut, in its application to the present case, is not consistent with the liberty of the citizen or with the freedom of interstate commerce, I dissent from the opinion and judgment of the court."

The last case to be mentioned involving freedom of contract in interstate commerce is that of Smith v. St. Louis and S. W. R. Co., 181 U. S. 248. Here was brought into question the constitutionality of a statute of Louisiana—a quarantine law—which forbade any shipment of cattle of any description from Texas into Louisiana, or from Louisiana into Texas, because of the existence of anthrax among the animals of Texas. The court sustained the law as a valid police regulation.

Justice Harlan, with whom concurred Justice White, objected to the sweeping scope of the law. Its inclusiveness, according to him, made undue restrictions upon interstate commerce. "The grounds of my dissent are these: (1) The railroad company was bound to discharge its duties as a carrier unless relieved therefrom by such quarantine regulations under the laws of Texas as were consistent with the Constitution of the United States. It could not plead in defense of its action the quarantine regulations adopted by the state sanitary commission and the proclamation of the governor of that state, if such regulations and proclamation were void under the Constitution of the United States. (2) The authority of the state to establish quarantine regulations for the protection of the health of its people does not authorize it to create an embargo upon all commerce involved in the transportation of live stock from Louisiana to Texas. The regulations and the governor's proclamation upon their face showed the existence of a certain cattle disease in one of the counties of Texas. If, under any circumstances, that fact could be the basis of an embargo upon the bringing into Texas from Louisiana of all live stock during a prescribed period, those circumstances should have appeared from the regulations and the proclamation referred to. On the contrary, there does not appear on the face of the transaction any ground whatever for establishing a complete embargo for any given period upon all transportation of live stock from Louisiana to Texas."

In other words, Justice Harlan could not see that there were sufficient grounds to cause the discontinuance of all shipments of cattle into Texas because of disease there. He could not see how sending cattle from Louisiana into Texas would bring disease from Texas into Louisiana, and hence he thought that such a restriction was an improper burden upon interstate commerce.

In considering the attitude of Justice Harlan to freedom of contract as a whole, the conclusion is inevitable that he was more liberal on this point than on almost any other. He magnified individual freedom greatly, and in so doing seemed to lose sight at times of the real working of the law. For instance, in Hooper v. California a doctrine such as he upheld would in practice have displaced the accepted position of insurance policies, and would have forced them into a rather anomalous category. They would not have been articles of commerce, and at the same time could not be subjected to effective regulation by the States. Thus they would have tended to slip out from under both national and state control.

Employers' Liability.—The case of Howard v. Illinois Central R. Co., 207 U. S. 463, brought before the Supreme Court the constitutionality of a statute of Congress, passed June 11, 1906, making employers liable for the injury or death of employees on railroad trains. That was the first employers' liability act passed by Congress, and was held to be unconstitutional as an attempt on the part of Congress to regulate intrastate as well as interstate commerce. The court spoke as follows: "Concluding, as we do, that the statute, whilst it embraces subjects within the authority of Congress to regulate commerce, also includes subjects not within its constitutional power, and that the two are so inter-blended in the statute that they are incapable of separation, we are of the opinion that the courts below rightly held the statute to be repugnant to the Constitution and non-enforceable."

Justices Moody, Harlan, Holmes, and McKenna dissented from this opinion. They asserted that though the statute could be so read as to make it include matters that were without the power of the general government to regulate, a narrower reading could and should have been given to it so as to make it constitutional. Justice Moody rendered an able dissent from this case, and Justice Harlan concurred in his views, but also gave a short dissenting opinion of his own. He said: " We do not concur in the interpretation of that act as given in the opinion delivered by Mr. Justice White, but think that the act, reasonably and properly interpreted, applies, and should be interpreted as intended by Congress to apply only to cases of interstate commerce and to employees who, at the time of the particular wrong or injury complained of, are engaged in such commerce, and not to domestic commerce or commerce completely internal to the State in which the wrong or injury occurred."

Beginning of the Interstate Commerce Commission.— There are two significant cases in which Justice Harlan differed from the court in its review of decisions rendered by the Interstate Commerce Commission. The first was the case of Texas and Pacific R. Co. v. Interstate Commerce Commission, 162 U. S. 197. Here the question was whether under the Interstate Commerce Act the railroad company could legally charge a cheaper rate for shipments of goods from foreign ports through the territory of the United States than it did between two equally distant places within the United States. The commission held that there had been an unlawful discrimination. In the Supreme Court it was argued that the Interstate Commerce Commission had erred in interpreting the statute of Congress by not considering circumstances which would have justified the railroad companies in making the distinction. The special circumstances under which they claimed justification were that since the freight vessels charged a cheaper rate for delivering goods from foreign ports to points along the Pacific coast, they were justified in putting the railroad rates so low as to draw the shipments over the land. This contention the Supreme Court upheld, reversing the decision of the circuit court: " The mere fact that the disparity between the through and local rates was considerable did not, of itself, warrant the court in finding that such disparity constituted an undue discrimination—much less did it justify the court in finding that the entire difference between the two rates was undue or unreasonable, especially as there was no person, firm, or corporation complaining that he or they had been aggrieved by such disparity." The case had been contested at the instigation of chambers of commerce.

As would naturally be supposed, Justice Harlan's contention was that such a decree legitimised partiality to foreign shippers as opposed to those at home. He contended that the Interstate Commerce Commission gave the only proper interpretation of the act of Congress, either as to its meaning or as to the intent of the legislators. He said: " If such discrimination by American railways, having arrangements with foreign companies, against goods, the product of American skill, enterprise and labor, is consistent with the act of Congress, then the title of that act should have been one to regulate commerce to the injury of American interests and for the benefit of foreign manufacturers and dealers."

He said further: " I am not much impressed by the anxiety which the railroad company professes to have for the interests of the consumers of foreign goods and products brought to this country under arrangement as to rates made by it with ocean transportation lines. We are dealing in this case only with a question of rates for the transportation of goods from New Orleans to San Francisco over the defendants' railroad. The consumers at San Francisco, those who may be supplied from that city, have no concern whether the goods reached them by the way of railroad from New Orleans, or by water around Cape Horn, or by route across the isthmus of Panama."

The last and most significant case regarding the early

powers of the Interstate Commerce Commission is that of the Interstate Commerce Commission v. Alabama Midland R. Co., 168 U. S. 144. This again was a case in which it was held that the commission had not given weight to material considerations.

The town of Troy, Alabama, claimed that it was discriminated against in railroad rates. On phosphate rock from a certain point to Troy the charge was $3.22 a ton, while from the same point to Montgomery, a longer distance, the charge was only $3 a ton. A similar rate was charged on cotton and various other commodities. Upon appeal to the Interstate Commerce Commission this was held to be discrimination, and the rates were ordered to be reduced to a certain point. Because of this reduction the case was taken by the railroad company into the circuit court of appeal, where the decision of the commission was overthrown, whereupon the commission appealed to the Supreme Court. The Supreme Court decided that in attempting to fix rates the commission had exceeded the powers granted to it by Congress. Furthermore, the court in this case went further than to attempt to determine whether the commission had rightly interpreted the statute of Congress. It justified this conduct by asserting that it had to investigate the circumstances in order to answer the question put by the Interstate Commerce Commission. It had been asked by the commission whether or not the decision made by the commission was right, and since the decision rested on the facts, the court had to investigate the facts to decide whether the commission had exceeded its jurisdiction or not. Having done this, it decided that the commission had exercised a power which it did not have, and furthermore asserted that the circumstances required a higher rate than the commission had set, hence the decision of the commission remained overthrown.

Justice Harlan disagreed with this decision because it apparently deprived the Interstate Commerce Commission of its ability to prevent discrimination in rates. He said:

"The Commission was established to protect the public against improper practices of transportation companies engaged in commerce among the several states. It has been left, it is true, with power to make reports and issue protests. But it has been shorn by judicial interpretation, of authority to do anything of an effective character. It is denied many of the powers which, in my judgment, were intended to be conferred upon it. Besides, the acts of Congress are now so construed as to place communities on the lines of interstate commerce at the mercy of competing railroad companies engaged in such commerce."

But however condemnable a situation may, for the time being, seem to be, it appears that somehow things right themselves in a government which is responsible to a healthy public opinion. At that time one of the most significant steps that had been taken to assure honest railroad rates must have seemed to Justice Harlan to have been blocked. The delay proved, however, to be only temporary, for since the above case was decided Congress has thought it wise so to amend the act establishing the Interstate Commerce Commission as to give it the power which the court in this case said that it did not have. In other words, Congress has said that it did mean to say what the court said that it did not mean to say, and what Justice Harlan contended was the only thing that it could very well have meant to say, namely, that the commission should determine what are fair rates for interstate lines to charge for the various articles of transportation.

Although the court alluded to the fact that the granting of the rate-making power to the Interstate Commerce Commission might be considered a delegation of legislative power, no definite point was made of it. This consideration did not seem to Justice Harlan to be a serious obstacle in the way of granting such a power to the Commission. Since the later amendment to the act of Congress, however, the judges seem to be unanimous in indicating that they do not consider this a delegation of the legislative power.

CHAPTER V

EQUAL PROTECTION OF THE LAWS

Race.—In discussing the question of the equal protection of the laws in reference to the negroes it will be necessary to bring into consideration cases which might have been dealt with exclusively under other subjects. There are seven cases in which this vexed question has arisen in one way or another: (1) The Civil Rights Cases, 109 U. S. 3; (2) Louisville, New Orleans and Texas R. Co. v. Mississippi, 133 U. S. 587; (3) Plessy v. Ferguson, 163 U. S. 537; (4) Giles v. Harris, 189 U. S. 475; (5) Hodges v. United States, 203 U. S. 1; (6) Berea College v. Kentucky, 211 U. S. 45; (7) Bailey v. Alabama, 219 U. S. 219. The first determined the position which the negroes should occupy in the States after the adoption of the thirteenth and fourteenth amendments, that is, that they should be citizens of the States and not wards of the nation. The second involved the constitutionality of the so-called Jim Crow laws from the standpoint of interstate commerce. The third passed upon the Jim Crow laws unde · the general provisions of the thirteenth and fourteenth amendments. The fourth refused to pass upon the constitutionality of the so-called disfranchisement provisions in the constitution of Alabama. The fifth and seventh involved the constitutionality of certain acts which were claimed to allow peonage in some of the Southern States. The sixth involved the constitutionality of a state law forbidding admission of negroes to Berea College, Kentucky. In every case the negro was denied the rights which he claimed.

The Civil Rights Cases will be discussed in more detail than the others, for in them is found the heart of the question as to the position which the negro was to occupy after the passage of the thirteenth and fourteenth amendments. There were five of these cases, but only four of them involved the main question. Two cases arose because of the refusal to admit negroes to hotels and two on account of the refusal to admit negroes to theatres on the same footing as other people; the other arose out of the refusal of a railway conductor to allow a colored woman to ride in the ladies' car. The contention of the plaintiffs was that these denials constituted violations of sections 1 and 2 of an act of Congress known as the Civil Rights Act, passed March 1, 1875, as appropriate legislation to enforce the rights which the negroes had acquired under the newly added amendments. The question, therefore, was whether the sections of the act were constitutional.

The argument of the court in declaring the sections unconstitutional may be summarized as follows: (1) In reply to the contention that the power of Congress to pass such a law was granted by the fourteenth amendment, the statement was made that, similar to the requirement that no State should pass any law impairing the obligation of contracts, it was state action of a particular character that was prohibited, and that individual invasion of individual rights was not the subject-matter of the amendment. A differentiation was thus made between the legislative powers of Congress under these amendments and those derived from the provisions of the Constitution which clothe Congress with plenary power of legislation over the whole subject-matter, as, for example, the regulation of interstate commerce. "In these cases, Congress has power to pass laws regulating subjects specified in every detail, and the conduct and transactions of individuals in every respect thereof. But where a subject is not submitted to the general legislative power of Congress, but is only submitted thereto for the purpose of rendering effective some prohibitions against particular State legislation or State action in reference to that subject, the power given is limited by its object, and any legislation by Congress in the matter must necessarily be corrective in character, adapted to counteract and redress the operation of such prohibited state laws or proceedings of State officers."

(2) Such legislation by Congress was not needed for the enforcement of the thirteenth amendment because that amendment is self-executing. "By its own unaided force and effect, it abolished slavery, and established universal freedom. Still legislation may be necessary and proper to meet all the various cases and circumstances to be affected by it, and to prescribe proper modes of redress for its violation in letter and in spirit, and such legislation may be primary and direct in its character; for the Amendment is not a mere prohibition on state laws establishing or upholding slavery, but an absolute declaration that slavery or involuntary servitude shall not exist in any part of the United States." The court admitted, therefore, that Congress had the right to pass any appropriate legislation for the obliteration and prevention of slavery, but denied that the refusal of admission to accommodations and privileges in all inns, public conveyances, and so on, subjected those persons to any form of servitude, or tended to fasten on them any badges of slavery. "It would be running the slavery argument into the ground, to make it apply to every act of discrimination which a person may see fit to make as to the guests he will entertain, or as to the people he will take into his coach or car, or admit to his concert or theatre, or deal with in other matters of intercourse or business. Innkeepers and public carriers, by the laws of all the States, so far as we are aware, are bound, to the extent of their facilities, to furnish proper accommodations to all unobjectionable persons who apply in good faith for them. If the laws themselves make any unjust discrimination, amenable to the 14th Amendment, Congress has full power to afford a remedy, under that Amendment and in accordance with it."

It is seen, therefore, that the argument of the court rested in the first place on the assumption that the fourteenth amendment gave Congress only the power of passing corrective legislation directed at state action, and that since the act in question was directed against individuals it could not be considered appropriate legislation for the enforcement of the provisions of the fourteenth amendment. In the second place, it was not appropriate legislation for the enforcement of the thirteenth amendment, for it had been aimed at some things which the appellants had attempted to characterize as badges of slavery, but which could not be termed such.

Justice Harlan's contentions in dissenting from these views may be briefly given as follows: First, he held that the freedom established by the thirteenth amendment involved more than exemption from actual slavery. It meant more than simply preventing one person from owning another as property. The people, in adding the thirteenth amendment to the Constitution, could not have intended to destroy simply the institution of slavery and then remit those who had been set free to the States which had held them in bondage, and expect those States to protect them in the rights which necessarily grew out of the freedom which those States did not desire them to have. "I do not contend that the 13th Amendment invests Congress with authority, by legislation, to define and regulate the entire body of civil rights which citizens enjoy, or may enjoy in the several States. But I hold that since slavery, as the court has repeatedly declared . . . was the moving force or principal cause of the adoption of that Amendment, and since that institution rested wholly upon the inferiority, as a race, of those held in bondage, their freedom necessarily involved immunity from, and protection against, all discrimination against them, because of their race, in respect of such civil rights as belong to freemen of other races."

Second, he held that it was not for the judiciary but for Congress to say what was appropriate legislation for the enforcement of the thirteenth and fourteenth amendments. "Under given circumstances, that which the court characterizes as corrective legislation might be deemed by Congress as appropriate and entirely sufficient. Under other circumstances primary direct legislation may be required. But it is for Congress, not the judiciary, to say that legislation is appropriate; that is, the best adapted to the end to be attained."

Another quotation along this same line will be pertinent: "With all respect for the opinion of others, I insist that the National Legislature may, without transcending the limits of the Constitution, do for human liberty and the fundamental rights of American citizenship, what it did, with the sanction of this court, for the protection of slavery and the rights of the master of fugitive slaves. If fugitive slave laws providing modes, and prescribing penalties whereby the master could seize and recover his fugitive slave, were legitimate exercises of an implied power to protect and enforce a right recognized by the Constitution, why shall the hands of Congress be tied, so that,—under an express power by appropriate legislation, to enforce a Constitutional provision granting citizenship—it may not, by means of direct legislation, bring the whole power of this Nation to bear upon States and their officers, and upon such individuals and corporations exercising public functions as assume to abridge, impair or deny rights confessedly secured by the supreme law of the land?"

This gives an insight into the most significant points developed by Justice Harlan. Other considerations were urged by him, but they were of less importance than these. His doctrine might be stated as follows: (1) Admission to hotels, places of amusement, and so forth, on equal footing with other citizens was a right that could not be denied to citizens without infringing their freedom; hence such refusals constituted badges of slavery, and could be punished under the section of the thirteenth amendment which gives Congress the right to enforce by appropriate legislation the provision against slavery or involuntary servitude. (2) It was absurd to take the slaves out of the hands of the

States, and soon thereafter give them back as free men to these same States, and expect them to be protected in their civil rights. The nation could not have meant to do so illogical a thing. And as simply the protection of the civil rights of negroes—or those who were once slaves—did not mean the taking by Congress of all civil rights of other citizens into its charge, such protection did not materially alter the nature of our institutions. No such alteration was intended by the newly added amendments. (3) It was not intended that the court should say what is meant by appropriate legislation. If Congress saw in certain acts badges and incidents of servitude or violations of the fourteenth amendment, it was not for the court to say what legislation Congress might choose to pass to remedy that condition; and a pronouncement by the court against the condition was judicial legislation. (4) Precedent showed that before the war Congress had, under an implied power, legislated so that owners of slaves could retain possession of their slaves; under an expressed power Congress should be able to secure freedmen in the possession of their rights.

When a fair examination is made of the decision and the dissent, the conclusion is plain that legally there is as much ground for one opinion as for the other. By a restricted and somewhat narrower interpretation of the amendments in question, the opinion of the court is logically sound. Justice Harlan's arguments do not refute the arguments of the court. His view is broader in some ways, and is based on a different line of reasoning. Both are sound constitutional doctrines, and the question was simply which of the two the majority of the court espoused. They upheld the former, and, of course, the decision went contrary to Justice Harlan's opinion. But since in this case the court decided the question upon the ground that the legislation in the Civil Rights Act was directed against individual action and was not corrective of state legislation and hence was unconstitutional, it will be interesting to follow the opinions that have been delivered as regards state acts.

The next case is Louisville, New Orleans and Texas R. Co. v. Mississippi, 133 U. S. 587. Since, however, this case was discussed fully under interstate and foreign commerce,[1] it need not be considered further at this point.

Probably the most typical case, after the Civil Rights Cases, that has arisen under the equal protection clause is that of Plessy v. Ferguson, 163 U. S. 537. This case also involved the constitutionality of a statute of a State requiring the separation of races on the trains. It was rested directly upon the equal protection clause, but brought into question the general purpose of the thirteenth and fourteenth amendments.

The court held the following opinion: (1) There was nothing to show that the statute required involuntary servitude: "A statute which implies merely a legal distinction between white and colored races—a distinction which is founded in the color of the two races, and which must always exist so long as white men are distinguished from the other race by color—has no tendency to destroy the legal equality of the two races, or to re-establish a state of involuntary servitude." (2) The statute was in no way in conflict with the fourteenth amendment: "The object of the amendment was undoubtedly to enforce absolute equality of the two races before the law, but in the nature of things it could not have been intended to abolish the distinctions based on color, or to enforce social, as distinguished from political, equality, or as commingling the two races upon terms unsatisfactory to either. . . . We consider the underlying fallacy of the plaintiff's argument to consist in the assumption that the enforced separation of the two races stamps the colored race with a badge of inferiority. If this be so it is not by reason of anything found in the act, but solely because the colored race chooses to put that construction upon it. The argument necessarily assumes that if, as has been more than once the case, and is not unlikely to be so again, the colored race should become the dominant power

---

[1] See pages 89–90.

in the state legislature, and should enact a law in precisely similar terms, it would thereby relegate the white race to an inferior position. We imagine that the white race, at least, would not acquiesce in this assumption." (3) The question as to the amount of negro blood necessary to stamp a person a negro was to be settled by the State. What the State pronounced in this regard would be held correct in the United States Supreme Court.

In opposition to these views Justice Harlan developed the following points: (1) The railroad, as a public highway, should not be directed or allowed to discriminate on account of race. "In respect of civil rights, common to all citizens, the Constitution of the United States does not, I think, permit any public authority to know the race of those entitled to be protected in the enjoyment of such rights. Every true man has pride of race, and under appropriate circumstances, when the rights of others, his equals before the law, are not to be affected, it is his privilege to express such pride and take such action based upon it as to him seems proper. But I deny that any legislative body or judicial tribunal may have regard to the race of its citizens when the civil rights of those citizens are involved. Indeed, such legislation as that here in question is inconsistent, not only with that equality of rights which pertains to citizenship, national and state, but with the personal liberty enjoyed by every one within the United States." (2) The thirteenth amendment does not permit the withholding or the deprivation of anything necessarily inhering in freedom. As that amendment had been found inadequate for the protection of the rights of those who had been in slavery, it was followed by the fourteenth, which added greatly to the dignity and glory of American citizenship. "Finally, and to the end that no citizen should be denied, on account of his race, the privilege of participating in the political control of his country it was declared by the 15th Amendment that 'the right of citizens of the United States to vote shall not be denied or abridged on account of race, color, or previous condition of servitude.'"

The following quotation will give the gist of the dissent: "It was said in argument that the statute of Louisiana does not discriminate against either race, but prescribes a rule applicable alike to white and colored citizens. But this argument does not meet the difficulty. Every one knows that the statute in question had its origin in the purpose, not so much to exclude the white persons from railroad cars occupied by blacks, as to exclude colored persons from coaches assigned to white persons. Railroad corporations of Louisiana did not make discrimination among whites in the matter of accommodation for travellers. The thing to accomplish was, under the guise of giving equal accommodation for whites and blacks to compel the latter to keep to themselves while travelling in railroad passenger coaches. No one would be so wanting in candor as to assert the contrary. . . .

"I am of opinion that the statute of Louisiana is inconsistent with the personal liberty of citizens, white and black, in that state, and hostile to both the spirit and letter of the Constitution of the United States. If laws of like character should be enacted in the several states of the Union, the effect would be in the highest degree mischievous. Slavery as an institution tolerated by law would, it is true, have disappeared from our country, but there would remain a power in the states, by sinister legislation, to interfere with the full enjoyment of the blessings of freedom."

The next case, Giles v. Harris, 189 U. S. 475, involved various provisions in the constitution of the State of Alabama which operated to disfranchise the negroes. The case had been dismissed from the circuit court because damages to the amount of two thousand dollars were not averred. It was appealed to the Supreme Court of the United States, where the point as to the amount averred was waived, and the case was argued on its merits. Although the court showed that it was not within the power of equity to grant relief, and not possible to assure the right to vote to the colored people in face of the opposition of the white population, it did not pass upon the constitutionality of the provisions in question. This case is discussed more fully in the chapter on jurisdiction of court.[2]

The next two cases involve the question of peonage in the Southern States. Hodges v. United States, 203 U. S. 1, was a review of a judgment in a lower federal court "convicting individual citizens of compelling negro citizens, by force and intimidation, to desist from performing their contracts of employment." It came by writ of error to the United States district court of Arkansas, where the decision was that interference with citizens to such an extent as to prevent them from contracting for their labor as they pleased was forbidden by the thirteenth amendment to the Constitution of the United States. The Supreme Court said that such an interference was not sufficient to be pronounced involuntary servitude as the words are used in the thirteenth amendment.

The arguments in the decision of the Supreme Court may be stated as follows: By a strict definition of slavery and involuntary servitude it was held that the lack of power to make or perform contracts was not embodied within the meaning of the thirteenth amendment. "It is said, however, that one of the disabilities of slavery, one of the *indicia* of its existence, was a lack of power to make or perform contracts, and that when these defendants, by intimidation and force, compelled the colored men named in the indictment to desist from performing their contracts, they, to that extent, reduced those parties to a condition of slavery,— that is, of subjection to the will of the defendants, and deprived them of a freeman's power to perform his contract. But every wrong done to an individual by another, acting singly or in concert with others, operates *pro tanto* to abridge some of the freedom to which the individual is entitled. A freeman has a right to be protected in his person from assault and battery. He is entitled to hold his property safe from trespass or appropriation; but no mere per-

---

[2] See pages 170–172.

sonal assault or trespass or appropriation operates to reduce the individual to a condition of slavery." Then follows a declaration that the thirteenth amendment did not intend to make the negroes wards of the nation, but only to give them citizenship and protect them against the abridgment of the privileges of citizenship by state action.

Justice Harlan did not agree with the arguments of the court in any particular. He claimed that a conspiracy forcibly to prevent citizens of African descent from contracting for their labor as they pleased infringed or violated a right or privilege, created by, derived from, or dependent upon the Constitution of the United States, because (1) the infringement of the right to contract for one's own labor is, within the meaning of the Constitution, slavery; (2) the thirteenth amendment not only abolished slavery, but authorized Congress to make this abolition effective by appropriate legislation; (3) Congress had passed such appropriate legislation by Par. 5508 of the Revised Statutes, which had been declared constitutional by the Supreme Court.

As is shown in another chapter, the case of Bailey v. Alabama, 211 U. S. 452, was dismissed on a technicality. This case is discussed elsewhere.[8] It is sufficient to say here that Justice Harlan in his dissent argued that the contention of the court was not well founded, and that the failure of the court to pass upon the constitutionality of the statute in question permitted discriminatory legislation.

Berea College v. Kentucky, 211 U. S. 45, involved the constitutionality of a law of Kentucky making it unlawful for negroes and whites to attend the same schools. In the Supreme Court this law was upheld as regarded its operation upon Berea College, a corporation of the State.

As will be shown later, Justice Harlan believed that a State had the right to prevent any corporation from entering its borders, but after a corporation had begun to do business there he did not think that because of this right the

---

[8] See pages 164–166.

State could impose any restriction it might please. This doctrine of his, combined with his strong desire to see the colored people get justice, brought forth a stinging dissent from him in the Berea College case. The spirit of his dissent here is not materially different from that in the other cases on this subject. The following quotation is typical: "In the eye of the law, the right to enjoy one's religious belief, unmolested by any human power, is no more sacred nor more fully or distinctly recognized than is the right to impart and receive instruction not harmful to the public. The denial of either right would be an infringement of the liberty inherent in the freedom secured by the fundamental law."

Justice Harlan's doctrine as to the position which the negroes should be allowed to occupy in our country may be stated as follows: He believed that they should occupy the position that historically they were intended to occupy by the thirteenth and fourteenth amendments. He believed that the law should be interpreted as it was meant and not as the court thought expedient and wise. Though it may be true that his relation to the negro in political matters may have made him more violent in his dissents, any one who will look fairly at the question must conclude that his doctrine was legally correct. And as time passes, and as both classes become better educated and broader in their views, it may be said that the tendency of the court is likely to be to interpret the laws largely as he thought they should have been interpreted, that is, as historically they were meant.

There are two cases representative of Justice Harlan's doctrine regarding legislation as to the Chinese immigrants in this country. They are Baldwin v. Franks, 120 U. S. 678, and United States v. Jung Ah Lung, 124 U. S. 621.

The first involved the following points: A group of men in California drove a Chinaman from his home and forbade his doing business in the town in which he had set up his laundry. These men were arraigned before the United

States circuit court and punished for having violated certain sections of the Civil Rights Act. Appeal was made by Baldwin upon writ of error to the Supreme Court of the United States, and here the decision of the circuit court was reversed.

In this case there were several questions to be answered, the most important of which was whether such acts were in violation of the following provisions of the revised statutes of Congress, being portions of the well-known Civil Rights Act: Sections 5508, 5519, and 5536. If they were violations of any of these sections, was the decision below constitutionally correct? In each point the court held as follows: The intent of Section 5519 was to impose a fine upon any person or group of persons who go upon the premises of another for the purpose of depriving him of the equal protection of the laws. That of Section 5508 was to make it criminal for two or more persons to threaten or in any way intimidate any citizen in the enjoyment of the rights secured to him by the Constitution. That of Section 5536 was to impose the same fine upon persons conspiring to destroy or hamper the force of the government of the United States. Section 5519 had already been declared unconstitutional, but the question was raised whether the same ruling would hold regarding aliens. The court held that the statute was not so worded as to be applicable to aliens. Section 5536 was likewise declared invalid. Section 5508, however, had been repeatedly declared constitutional. The question was, therefore, did this section apply to this particular case? The court answered this question by saying that the statute applied to *citizens* and not to *persons*, therefore it could not have been meant to apply to aliens.

The following quotation from Justice Harlan's dissent will indicate his answers to the arguments of the court: "It would seem from the decision in this case, that if Chinamen, having a right, under treaty, to remain in our country, are forcibly driven from their places of business, the Government of the United States is without power in its own courts to protect them against such violence, or to punish those who, in this way subject them to ill treatment. If this be so, as to Chinamen lawfully in the United States, it must be equally true as to citizens, or subjects of every other foreign Nation, residing or doing business here under the sanction of treaties with their respective governments. I do not think that such is the present state of the law."

In reference to the assertion of the court that the act did not apply to aliens, he said that since further on in the act the word "another" instead of "citizen" occurred, Congress must have had in mind any other person, whether a citizen or not.

He again contended that in spite of the previous decisions regarding Section 5519, it was constitutional as appropriate legislation to secure rights guaranteed under the thirteenth and fourteenth amendments. "If Congress, upon looking over the whole ground, determined that an effectual and appropriate mode to secure such protection was to proceed directly against a combination of individuals, who sought, by conspiracy or by violent means, to defeat the enjoyment of the right given by the Constitution, I do not see upon what ground the court can question the validity of legislation to that end." That is, of course, but a reiteration of his disapproval of the declaration of unconstitutionality in the Civil Rights Cases. Justice Harlan's dissent from this case, therefore, was simply a call to the nation to stand by its treaty obligations to aliens regardless of race or other considerations.

The case of the United States v. Jung Ah Lung contains what appears to be a departure from Justice Harlan's usual mode of dissent, but a close examination shows that it was not a departure. The case in question came up from the United States circuit court for the district of California. It was an appeal to review the decision of this court issuing a writ of habeas corpus to immigration authorities who held a Chinaman because of his inability to produce a certificate which would have shown that he was a laborer in this country prior to the passage of the Chinese exclusion acts, and which would have, therefore, given him the right to readmission into this country. It appeared that Jung Ah Lung had been captured by pirates and had been robbed of this certificate, which according to the law he was required to produce before he could be allowed to reenter this country. The circuit court denied the claim of the immigration officials that their decision was final, and gave the Chinaman a hearing.

As it appeared from other evidence satisfactory to the court that he was the same man to whom this certificate had been issued, and that, in the light of every consideration except the production of the certificate, he was entitled to enter, the circuit court ordered his release. This order the Supreme Court of the United States upheld.

Justice Harlan, with Justices Field and Lamar concurring, contended that the action of the circuit court was wrong. The law expressly stated that the certificate should be produced, and admission without it was illegal. The reason for their contention was, in the first place, that admission through one port ought not to have been allowed on any condition that could not be allowed in another port. Immigration laws in order to be constitutional must be uniform. Since the defendant could not have been admitted under the same circumstances through any port except the one from which he departed, he ought not to have been admitted through that one.

In the second place, since the law read that "said certificate shall be the only evidence permissible to establish his right to re-enter," the court did not have a right to accept any other evidence. "If appellee's certificate was forcibly taken from him by a band of pirates, while he was absent, that is his misfortune. That fact ought not to defeat what was manifestly the intention of the legislative branch of the Government. Congress, in the Act of 1882, said, in respect to a Chinese laborer who was here when the treaty of 1880 was made, and who afterwards left the country, that the 'proper evidence' of his right to go and come from the United States was the certificate he received from the collector of customs at the time of his departure, and that he should be entitled to re-enter 'upon producing and delivering such certificate' to the collector of customs of the district at which he seeks to re-enter; while this court decides that he may re-enter the United States without producing such certificate, and upon satisfactory evidence that he once had it, but was unable to produce it. As by the very terms of the act, a Chinese laborer, who was here on November 17, 1880, is not excepted from the provision absolutely suspending the coming of that class to this country for a given number of years, unless he produces to the collector the certificate issued to him, we cannot assent to the judgment of the court."

The loss of that certificate would seem to be similar to the loss of a ticket of any kind. As a matter of practice no one assumes that if a person has lost his ticket he will be allowed to ride on a train or got to a theatre. In the same way there seems to be no reason why any one should have assumed that a Chinaman could have been readmitted to this country without his certificate of admission.

There is one case of particular interest regarding attempts at discrimination against Indians. There seem to be few attempts to deny the equal protection of the laws to them, and this is an interesting fact in its relation to race prejudice. Though it must be admitted that the Indians have not at all times been fairly dealt with in other respects by the white people, it cannot be said that the race prejudice against them has been strong. It is an interesting observation that the presence of any white blood in their veins tends to classify them as white rather than red men; and people possessing Indian blood are often proud of the fact.

The case in question, however, does contain an element of denial of the equal protection of the laws. The case is Elk v. Wilkins, 112 U. S. 94. It came by writ of error from the United States district court for Nebraska, and arose because of the fact that a registration officer had denied to the Indian the right to register as an elector of the city of Omaha. Elk, the Indian, had severed his tribal connections, and had taken up his abode among the white citizens of Nebraska. Having been denied the right to vote, and the necessary requirements being present for the recognition of the suit by the district court, he entered suit against Wilkins, the registration officer, on the plea that he had been denied rights granted to him under the fourteenth and fifteenth amendments of the United States Constitution,—under the fourteenth amendment in that he was born in the United States and hence was a citizen thereof, and under the fifteenth amendment in that he had been denied the right to vote because of race. The lower court decided against him, and the decision was sustained in the Supreme Court.

The reason for this decision was that Indians could not become citizens except through the regular process of naturalization. Since this process had not been complied with, the Indian in question was not a citizen. Nor did the fact that he was born in the United States alter the situation. The reason for such a decree was the fact that Congress had in all respects dealt with the Indians as if they were aliens, and had passed no statute making citizens of them. Hence the denial of the right to vote did not need to be considered.

Justice Harlan in his dissent established the fact that the Indian in question had taken up his abode in the State in such a way as to be subject to taxation. This point established, he showed that the words "excluding Indians not taxed" as inserted in the fourteenth amendment recognized that there were a number of Indians in the States who were taxed, and that these were not excluded from citizenship, but were impliedly included. From this, therefore, he concluded that Indians in the position which Elk occupied were recognized as citizens by the fourteenth amendment. This assertion he reinforced by showing by quotations that the men who drew up the amendment meant it that way. Furthermore, he showed that in the act of Congress passed in 1886 regulating the relations with Indians the same phrase was used and with the same meaning.

The following conclusion is significant: "Born, therefore, in the territory, under the dominion and within the jurisdictional limits of the United States, plaintiff has acquired, as was his undoubted right, a residence in one of the States, with her consent, and is subject to taxation and to all other burdens imposed by her upon residents of every race. If he did not acquire national citizenship on abandoning his tribe and becoming subject by residence in one of the States to the complete jurisdiction of the United States, then the 14th Amendment, has wholly failed to accomplish, in respect to the Indian race, what we think was intended by it; and there is still in this country a despised and rejected class of persons, with no nationality whatever; who, born in our country, owing no allegiance to any foreign power, and subject, as residents of the States, to all the burdens of government, are yet not members of any polit ical community nor entitled to any of the rights, privileges or immunities of citizens of the United States."

It may be noted that this situation was alleviated by an act of Congress, passed in 1887, which made citizens of such men whether they wished citizenship or not.

Corporations.—Since the case of Paul v. Virginia, 8 Wall. 168, which determined the fact that corporations are citizens in the constitutional sense, was decided prior to Justice Harlan's appointment as associate justice, it is not possible to say what would have been exactly his view on this subject. There is, however, in the case of Atchison, Topeka, and Santa Fé R. Co. v. Matthews, 174 U. S. 96, an interesting expression of his opinion on this general subject, but since this case did not present the question squarely to the court, his constitutional doctrine on the subject cannot be deduced.

This case came from the supreme court of Kansas, and involved the constitutionality of a statute of that State which required that a railroad company, in case of suit for damages against it by an injured person, should pay, in addition to the damages awarded by the court, the attorneys' fees of the plaintiff. One of the questions raised was whether the statute did not discriminate against the railroad company in that it stipulated that the company should pay the fees if the suit went against them, and did not force the plaintiffs to pay the fees if the suit went in favor of the company. The court, nevertheless, upheld the statute on the ground that the classification was just in that it was made because of the nature of the business, the railway business being one which people enter at their peril.

Though Justice Harlan's argument in this case may not seem fair, it is extremely interesting. After reviewing the decision in Gulf, Colorado and Santa Fé R. Co. v. Ellis, 165 U. S. 150, he said: "If the opinions in the *Ellis Case* and in this case be taken together, the state of the law seems to be this:

"I. A state *may not* require a railroad company sued for negligently killing an animal to pay to the plaintiff, in addition to the damages proved and the ordinary costs, a reasonable attorney's fee, when it does not allow the corporation when its defense is sustained to recover a like attorney's fee from the plaintiff.

"2. A state *may* require a railroad company sued for and adjudged liable to damages arising from fire caused by the operation of its road, to pay to the plaintiff, in addition to the damages proved and the ordinary costs, a reasonable attorney's fee, even if it does not allow the corporation when successful in its defense to recover a like attorney's fee from the plaintiff. . . .

"Having assented in the *Ellis Case* to the first proposition, I cannot give my assent to the suggestion that the second proposition is consistent with the principles there laid down. Placing the present case beside the former case, I am not astute enough to perceive that the Kansas statute is consistent with the Fourteenth Amendment, if the Texas statute be unconstitutional."

This gives the main contention in his dissent. But there is another that should be noted, namely, that the statute did not apply to all corporations, but only to railroad companies: "Taken in connection with the principles of general law recognized in that state, that statute, although not imposing any special duties upon railroad companies, in effect says to the plaintiffs, Matthews and Trudell, the owners of the elevator property—indeed it says in effect to every individual citizen, and for that matter every corporation in the state: 'If you are sued by a railroad corporation for damages done to its property by fire caused by *your* negligence, or in the use of *your* property, the recovery against you shall not exceed the damages proved and the ordinary costs of the suit. But if your property is destroyed by fire caused by the operation of the railroad belonging to the same corporation, and you succeed in an action brought to recover damages, you may recover, in addition to the damages proved and the ordinary costs of suit, a reasonable attorney's fee; and if you fail in such action no attorney's fee shall be taxed against you.' In my judgment, such discrimination against a litigant is not consistent with the equal protection of the laws secured by the Fourteenth Amendment."

When it is considered what the court really did in these two cases, there is small wonder that there was objection on the part of some one. In one instance a Texas statute had been declared unconstitutional in a suit in which an individual had sought the benefit of its operation, while in the second instance a partnership firm had been granted the protection of the same sort of law that had been declared unconstitutional in Texas.

One of the most significant cases on the subject of taxation of corporations, the Fire Association of Philadelphia

v. New York, 119 U. S. 110, came by writ of error from the supreme court of New York. A law of New York required that a fire-insurance corporation chartered in another State should pay a greater tax than domestic corporations did. The question to be answered was whether the statute was unconstitutional in that it denied to such corporations the equal protection of the laws.

The argument of the court in this case can best be given in a single quotation: " The Pennsylvania corporation came into the State of New York to do business, by the consent of the State, under the act of 1853, with a license granted for a year, and has received such license annually, to run for a year. It is within the State for any given year under such license, and subject to the conditions prescribed by the statute. The State having the power to exclude entirely, has the power to change the conditions of admission at any time, for the future, . . . and the foreign corporation until it pays such license fee is not admitted within the State or within its jurisdiction. It is outside, at the threshold, seeking admission, with consent not yet given. The Act of 1865 had been passed when the corporation first established an agency within the State. The amendment of 1875 changed the Act of 1865 only by giving to the superintendent the power of remitting the fees and charges required to be collected by then existing laws. Therefore, the corporation was at all times, after 1872, subject, as a prerequisite to its power to do business in New York, to the same license fee its own State might thereafter impose on New York companies doing business in Pennsylvania. By going into the State of New York in 1872, it assented to such prerequisites as a condition of its admission within the jurisdiction of New York. It could not be of right within such jurisdiction, until it should receive the consent of the State to its entrance therein under the new provisions, such a consent could not be given until the tax, as a license fee for the future, should be paid."

Thus it is seen that the argument of the court was, briefly, this: Since a corporation is a citizen in a different sense from an ordinary person, different requirements may be made for it. Since a State may forbid a corporation to do business at all within its limits, it may put any restrictions it pleases upon its doing business there.

Justice Harlan agreed that a State had a right to exclude a corporation from its bounds, but he would not accept the added corollary that the State could, because of this power of exclusion, subject the corporation doing business within its limits to any restrictions it might choose.

He said: "Even if it were conceded that a State, which provides for the organization, under her own laws, of corporations for the transaction of every kind of business, could arbitrarily exclude from her limits similar corporations from the remaining States, and declare all contracts made within her jurisdiction with corporations from other States, to be void—concessions to be made only for the purposes of this case—it would not follow that she could subject corporations of other States, doing business within her limits under a license from the proper department, to higher taxes than she imposes upon other corporations of the same class from the remaining States."

Coming more nearly to the point at issue, he said: "The denial of the equal protection of the laws may occur in various ways. It will most often occur in the enforcement of laws imposing taxes. An individual is denied the equal protection of the laws if his property is subjected by the State to higher taxation than is imposed upon like property of other individuals in the same community. So, a corporation is denied that protection when its property is subjected by the State, under whose laws it is organized, to more burdensome taxation than is imposed upon other domestic corporations of the same class. So, also, a corporation of one State, doing business, by its agents, in another State by the latter's consent, is denied the equal protection of the laws, if its business there is subjected to higher taxation than is imposed upon the business of like corporations of other States. These propositions seem to me to be indisputable. They are necessarily involved in the concession that corporations, like individuals, are entitled to the equal protection of the laws."

He said further: "It would seem to me to be the result of the decision in this case, that New York may prescribe such varying rates of taxation upon insurance corporations of the remaining thirty-seven States, within her jurisdiction, as she chooses—the rate for corporations from each State differing from the rate established for corporations of the same class from all other States, and the rate in respect to corporations of other States being higher than she imposes upon her own corporations of the same class. Such legislation would be a species of commercial warfare by one State against the others, and would be hostile to the whole spirit of the Constitution, and particularly the Fourteenth Amendment, securing to all persons within the jurisdiction of the respective States the equal protection of the laws."

In this case is seen the first promulgation of Justice Harlan's doctrine that wherever a corporation has a right to do business it has a right to the equal protection of the laws. His reason for holding to this doctrine is well stated in the last quotation given, namely, that if such discrimination were allowed it would give rise to a condition of commercial warfare that would be unwholesome in many ways.

This same doctrine was announced in his dissent from People, ex rel. Parke, Davis, and Co. v. Roberts, 171 U. S. 658. This case, however, presented the question in a slightly different form. Here arose the question of the constitutionality of a statute of the State of New York which imposed a higher tax on corporations which manufactured their goods outside of the State and sent them there to be sold than was imposed on either New York or out-of-the-State corporations which operated plants within the State. The claim was made by Parke, Davis, and Company, an out-of-the-State corporation which wished to do business in the State of New York without setting up an establishment in the State, that this law was unconstitutional in that it denied to them the equal protection of the laws.

A brief quotation will make clear the argument of the court: "It is said that the operation of that portion of this taxing law, which exempts from a business tax corporations which are wholly engaged in manufacturing within the State of New York, is to encourage manufacturing corporations which seek to do business in that State to bring their plants into New York. Such may be the tendency of the legislation, but so long as the privilege is not restricted to New York corporations, it is not perceived that thereby any ground is afforded to justify the intervention of the Federal courts."

Justice Harlan's reply to this assertion is very convincing. He said, after an extended discussion of previous cases: "I am unable to reconcile the opinion and judgment in the present case with the principles announced in the above cases. A tax upon the capital employed by a manufacturing corporation or company is *pro tanto* a tax upon the goods manufactured by it. If this be not so, there are many expressions in the former opinions of this court which should be withdrawn or modified. A corporation or company wholly engaged in manufacture in New York has an advantage, in the sale of its goods in the markets of that state, over a corporation or company manufacturing like goods in other states, if the former is altogether exempted from taxation in respect of its franchise or business, and the latter subjected to taxation of its franchise or business, measured by the amount of its capital employed in New York. That state may undoubtedly tax capital employed within its limits by corporations or companies of other states, but it cannot impose restrictions that will necessarily prevent such corporations or companies from selling their goods in New York upon terms of equality with corporations or companies wholly engaged there in manufacturing goods of like kind. . . . In my judgment, this statute cannot be sustained in its application to the plaintiff in error without recognizing the power of New York, so far as the Federal Constitution is concerned, to enact such statutes as will by their necessary operation amount to a tariff protecting goods manufactured in that state against competition in the market there with goods manufactured in other states. And if such legislation as is embodied in the statute in question is held to be consistent with the Federal Constitution, why may not New York, while exempting from taxation the franchises or business of corporations or companies wholly engaged in carrying on their manufacturing in that State, put such taxation upon the franchise or business of corporations or companies doing business in that State, but not wholly engaged in manufacture there, as will amount to an absolute prohibition upon the sale in New York of goods manufactured in other states? . . . I had supposed that the Constitution of the United States had established absolute free trade among the States of the Union, and that freedom from injurious discrimination in the markets of any state, against goods manufactured in this country, was a vital principle of constitutional law."

The case of Fidelity Mutual Life Insurance Co. v. Mettler, 185 U. S. 308, contains a similar point. In this case the court upheld a statute of Texas which directed that life and health insurance companies which should default in the payment of their policies should pay as damages, in addition to the face of the policy, twelve per cent of the original amount, together with reasonable attorneys' fees that might have been made necessary in the collection of the money due to be paid. The claim was made that this statute was unconstitutional in that it discriminated against health and life insurance companies as opposed to other insurance companies, and therefore denied to them the equal protection of the laws. The court held that the statute was constitutional in that it was a condition imposed by a State upon the right of a corporation to do business within its borders.

In his dissent from this case is stated even more clearly Justice Harlan's doctrine as to the constitutional rights of a corporation doing business in any State: " It is one thing for a state to forbid a particular foreign corporation, or a particular class of foreign corporations, from doing business at all within its limits. It is quite another thing for a state to admit or license foreign corporations to do business within its limits, and then subject them to some statutory provision that is repugnant to the Constitution of the United States. If a corporation, doing business in Texas under its licence or with its consent, insists that a particular statute or regulation is in violation of the Constitution of the United States and cannot therefore be enforced against it, the State need only reply—such seems to be the logical result of the present decision—that the statute or regulation is a condition of the right of the corporation to do business in the state, and, whether constitutional or not, must be respected by the corporation. Corporations created by the several states are necessary to the conduct of the business of the country; and it is a startling proposition that a state may permit a corporation to do business within its limits, and by that act acquire the right to subject the corporation to regulations that may be inconsistent with the supreme law of the land."

It was a good while, however, before the other members of the court seemed to see his point. They had gone on the assumption that a whole is the sum of its parts, whereas the proposition which they were facing was not one of geometry, but of business. The analogy did not, therefore, hold. In the case of Western Union Telegraph Co. v. Kansas, 216 U. S. 1, they finally saw this, and Justice Harlan was himself called upon to deliver the opinion of the court. He found opportunity to express in an affirmative way his long cherished doctrine: " The exaction from a foreign telegraph company for the benefit of the permanent school fund, under the authority of Kan. Gen. Stat. 1901, p. 280, of a ' charter fee ' of a given per cent of its entire authorized capital stock, as a condition of continuing to do local business in the state, is invalid under the commerce and due-process-of-law clauses of the Federal Constitution, as necessarily amounting to a burden and tax on the company's interstate business and on its property located or used outside the state." Though this decision was delivered under the commerce and due process clauses, and not under the equal protection provision, the principle was the same.

CHAPTER VI

JURISDICTION OF COURTS

Removal of Suits.—The question seems to be settled that if a case has been decided in a state court it is then too late to remove it into a lower federal court. But some very interesting points come up in determining when the question at issue in a suit may be termed res judicata. A typical instance of this kind occurred in the case of Congress and Empire Spring Co. v. Knowlton, 103 U. S. 49. Here the Supreme Court affirmed a decision of the United States circuit court for the northern district of New York, which had asserted that money paid on an illegal contract could on certain conditions be recovered. The suit might have been brought in the federal court because of diversity of citizenship, and the question before the Supreme Court was whether there was sufficient evidence that the case had been decided in the New York court to prevent the lower federal court from taking jurisdiction and deciding the case regardless of any other decision. The Supreme Court said that there was not, but Justice Harlan said that there was.

The reason why the court held that this suit had not been decided was that there was not sufficient evidence on the record to show that fact. "It is suggested by the counsel for the plaintiff in error, that the Court of Appeals of the State of New York has in this identical suit, upon the same state of facts, adjudicated the rights of the parties, and this court ought to consider the questions raised in this case as *res judicata.*

"The reply to this suggestion is, that it nowhere appears in the record that this case was ever before the Court of Appeals, or that it was ever decided by any court except the United States Circuit Court for the Northern District of New York, from which the case has been brought to this court on error. We cannot consider facts not brought to our notice by the record."

Justice Harlan knew that when the court desired to do so it sometimes considered facts not brought to its notice by the record, and he contended that on this occasion the evidence was sufficient. "It is, in my judgment," he said, "an immaterial circumstance, that the present transcript does not contain the proceedings had in the Commission of Appeals. An examination of the case reported in 57 N. Y. shows beyond question, that it is the identical case now before us; at any rate, that it was a case between the same parties who are now before us, and that it involved the same issues that are here presented for our determination. We know that the adjudication in that court was long prior to the removal of this case into the federal court. We know also that the questions decided in the Circuit Court, and which we are now asked to determine, have been once passed upon, between the same parties, in a court of competent jurisdiction. All this plainly appears upon the face of the decision reported in 57 N. Y. The defendants in error should not, therefore, be permitted to escape the legal effect of that decision by a removal of the case into the Circuit Court of the United States." This comment Justice Harlan had previously reinforced by the assertion that the "learned District Judge, who tried the case in the Circuit Court, opened his opinion, which is part of the transcript, with the statement that 'the case comes here by removal from the State court, after a decision adverse to the plaintiff by the Commission of Appeals, reversing the judgment of the Supreme Court in favor of plaintiff, and ordering a new trial.' He then proceeds to determine the case upon principles of law different from those announced by the Commission of Appeals."

Justice Harlan's contention here was that even if the record itself did not show that the case had been tried before, extensive evidence showing that the case had been tried should be accepted as determining the fact.

Another case directly connected with the subject of removal is that of Fisk v. Henarie, 142 U. S. 459. Here the court decided that an application for removal into the United States circuit court was made too late. The case had been pending in the state courts from 1883 to 1887. It had been tried three times in the lower state courts with no satisfactory results. It had been appealed to the state supreme court and remanded to the lower courts for retrial, after which the case was held up and postponed so often that it was practically impossible to have a final judicial determination in the state courts.

The suit involved the amount of $60,000, and there was diversity of citizenship. The question at issue for the Supreme Court to decide was whether the Judiciary act of 1887, which sought to reduce the number of cases to be heard by the United States circuit court, so restricted the field as to make it impossible for the federal court to give relief. The syllabus of the case gives the decree of the court: "Under the Act of March 3, 1887, a cause may be removed from a state court into the U. S. Circuit Court at any time before the trial thereof, on the ground of prejudice or local influence; after a cause has been tried three times in the state court an application for removal is too late."

Justice Harlan's contention was that the setting of such a limit was contrary to what Congress meant by the statute passed in 1887. He thought that further procedure might be necessary before it could be ascertained whether local prejudice would thwart the dealing out of justice. "The fact of prejudice or local influence may be established by overwhelming evidence; still under the decision of the court, there can be no removal if the application for removal be not made before the first trial. We do not mean to say that when a trial is in progress that the cause may be removed before its termination, even upon the ground of prejudice or local influence. But, if at the time the application is made the cause is not on trial and is undetermined, that is, has not been effectively tried, the Act of 1887, in our judgment, authorizes a removal, on proper showing, upon the ground of prejudice or local influence, although there may have been a trial, resulting in a verdict which has been set aside. . . .

"Congress could hardly have intended to give the defendant citizen of another State simply the time between his answering or pleading, and the calling of his case for the first trial thereof, to determine whether he should apply for a removal upon the ground of prejudice or local influence. In our judgment, it meant to give the right of removal, upon such ground, at any time, when the case is not actually on trial, and when there is in force no judgment fixing the rights of the parties in the suit. If a case is open *for* trial, on the merits, an application for its removal before that trial commences is made 'before the trial thereof.' In our opinion, the interpretation adopted by the court defeats the purpose which Congress had in view for the protection of persons sued elsewhere than in the State of which they are citizens."

By contrasting the two cases discussed we may deduce Justice Harlan's doctrine that anything that has actually been decided is res judicata, but that which has not been decided is not res judicata. The length of time during which it has been pending is not to be considered, as long as the case is not actually on trial.

In the case of Railroad Co. v. Ide, 114 U. S. 52, the Supreme Court decided, curiously enough, that in a suit between a citizen or citizens of one State and a citizen or citizens of another State diversity of citizenship does not necessarily exist. In order that diversity of citizenship, within the meaning of the Constitution, shall exist, all the parties plaintiff or complainant must be of different citizenship from that of all of the defendants. The diversity must be complete. This doctrine Justice Harlan opposed. He dissented in Railroad Co. v. Ide without giving grounds for his dissent, but when the question came up again in Pirie v. Tvedt, 115 U. S. 41, he broke his silence. This case arose between citizens of Minnesota on the one hand and citizens of Illinois and of Minnesota on the other. The court held that this case was governed by that of Railroad Co. v. Ide, and that the diversity of citizenship was not such as could be termed diversity in the constitutional sense.

Justice Harlan asserted that there was diversity of citizenship, and that even if a decree could not be rendered against those parties who were citizens of Minnesota, it could be rendered against the citizens of Illinois. "Had the suit been only against the defendants who are citizens of Illinois, as it might have been, the right of the latter to remove it into the Circuit Court of the United States would not be questioned. But it seems, by the present decision, that their right of removal has been defeated by the act of the plaintiffs in waiting in uniting with them as defendants, citizens of Minnesota, against whom, as is conceded, it was not necessary to introduce any evidence whatever in order to entitle the plaintiffs to a judgment against the other defendants. As in most, if not in all States the local statutes dispense with the verification of the pleadings in action of tort, this convenient device will be often employed. When, for instance, a citizen of New York has a cause of action, sounding in damages, against a citizen of New Jersey, who happens to go within the jurisdiction of the former State, the plaintiff can join a citizen of New York as a co-defendant, charging them jointly with the liability to him for damages claimed. And when the citizen of New Jersey asks a removal of the suit to the federal court, he is met with the suggestion that it is for the plaintiff, in his discretion to sue him separately, or jointly with others. Upon his application to remove the cause, the state court may not institute a preliminary inquiry as to whether the plaintiff had, in fact, a cause of action against the defendant citizen of New York. It is not for that court, in advance, to determine the good faith of the plaintiff in making a citizen of New York a co-defendant with the citizen of New Jersey. The removal statutes make no provision for such an inquiry, and the state court, by the decision just rendered, must look alone to the course of action as set out in the petition or complaint. When, in the case supposed, the evidence is concluded, and it appears that there is, in fact, no cause of action against the defendant citizen of New York, it is too late for the removal to occur; for, it must be had, if at all, before the suit could be tried in the State court."

Justice Harlan opposed this differentiation in diversity of citizenship, which the court made, on account of a practical consideration as well as because of proper constitutional construction. He believed that diversity of citizenship ought not to have been so interpreted as to enable the unscrupulous to play with the law.

Another case in which arose the very interesting question as to what constitutes diversity of citizenship of corporations is St. Louis and San Francisco R. Co. v. James, 161 U. S. 545. Here one Etta James sued to recover damages for the death of her husband, who was killed while a fireman upon that railroad. She was a citizen of Missouri, and the railroad company was also a citizen of Missouri, being a corporation chartered by that State. She contended that inasmuch as the company was doing business under the laws of Arkansas it was also a citizen of that State, and that there was therefore diversity of citizenship. The court decided that a corporation could not be a citizen of two States at the same time, and since it was chartered in Missouri, the company was a Missouri citizen, and there was therefore no diversity of citizenship.

Justice Harlan dissented. According to his doctrine, a corporation could under certain conditions be considered a citizen of two States. Since in this case the railroad company had agreed to submit to the laws of Arkansas for the privilege of doing business there, and since the laws of that State stipulated that every railroad company that did business within that State, whether chartered elsewhere or not, should become a citizen of that State, this company had properly to be considered as a citizen of Arkansas as well as of Missouri, and if the Arkansas corporation was sued by a citizen of another State there was diversity of citizenship.

"At first blush," he says, "it may seem strange that the plaintiff did not sue the Missouri corporation in one of the courts of Missouri. But that cannot affect the jurisdiction of the court below, if the defendant is an Arkansas corporation. And her right to a judgment cannot be denied, if the Arkansas corporation is liable for injuries caused, in Missouri, by the negligence of the Missouri corporation. It may be that the line in Missouri is covered by mortgages for very large amounts, so that a judgment against the Missouri corporation would be of no real value. That perhaps is the reason why the plaintiff brought suit against the Arkansas corporation. But, as already said, this view is not at all material on the present hearing."

Closely allied to the matter of diversity of citizenship is the question as to where the suit may properly be brought. This point came out very emphatically in the case of Macon Grocery Co. v. Atlantic Coast Line R. Co., 215 U. S. 501. Here was involved an attempt on the part of certain shippers of Georgia to prevent a conjoint action of several railroad companies to put into operation an increase in freight rates. The action was brought in the United States circuit court for the southern district of Georgia on the ground of diversity of citizenship. The court held that such a suit could not be conducted in the federal court for that district, and had to be brought in the district of one of the corporations. This decision was based upon the act of Congress of 1888, which, the court asserted, provided that "no civil suit shall be brought . . . in any other district than that whereof he [the defendant] is an inhabitant, but where the jurisdiction is founded only on the fact that the action is between citizens of different states, suit shall be brought only in the district of the residence of either the plaintiff or the defendant."

Justice Harlan differed from the court as to its interpretation of the Act of 1888, and emphasized the lack of wisdom of the decree. In referring to the act he made the following comment: "I recognize the fact that the act of 1888 was not drawn with precision. But I am of opinion that, as the act gives the circuit court original jurisdiction, concurrent with the courts of the several states, 'of all suits of a civil nature, at common law or in equity, where the matter in dispute exceeds, exclusive of interest and costs, the sum or value of $2,000 . . . in which there shall be a controversy between citizens of different states,' the intention of Congress would be best effectuated by holding that the jurisdiction of the circuit court is not excluded, in a controversy between citizens of different states, simply because the plaintiff, who sued in the Federal court held in the state of his residence, asserts a Federal right and seeks to have it protected against the illegal acts of the defendant, a citizen of another state; provided, always, that the defendant, if a corporation of another state, may, through agents conducting its business in the state where the suit is brought, be reached by the process of the court, and subjected to its authority. The presence in the case of a Federal right asserted by the plaintiff ought not to prejudice him, and does not, I think, alter the fact that the controversy is one of which a circuit court may take cognizance, because it is a controversy between citizens of different states."

Justice Harlan also differed from the court on other grounds. He contended that, to start with, the complaint should have been made to the Interstate Commerce Commission, where the question would almost certainly have been once for all settled. "This, I think, is all that need have been said; for, whatever interpretation was given to the judiciary act of 1888 . . . the circuit court would have been required, under the case just cited [B. & O. R. Co. v.

United States, 215 U. S. 481], to decline jurisdiction. But the court, in its wisdom, does not refer to this view of the case, and deems it necessary to determine whether the plaintiffs, citizens of Georgia, may, under the judiciary act of 1888, considered alone, invoke the jurisdiction of the circuit court, held in that state, against the defendant corporations of other states."

This quotation shows sufficiently well the grounds of Justice Harlan's dissent. Since the Interstate Commerce Commission had been established for the express purpose of passing upon such a contention as this, he saw no reason why all jurisdiction other than that should not have been excluded and the case remanded for determination there. The court was uselessly contending for something that was not necessarily to be considered, and avoiding that which made the case very simple. Nevertheless, he proceeded to reply to the contentions of the court, and to show that a wiser interpretation of the act would have been to allow the suit to be brought into the federal court at the home of the plaintiff as well as at that of any of the corporations.

It may appear that the cases just considered turn on questions of statutory construction rather than of constitutional right. They are, however, significant as evidencing the strong desire on the part of Justice Harlan to secure to the individual when possible the right of resort to federal courts.

The Meaning of Federal Immunity.—There are two very significant cases in which Justice Harlan differed from the court in its interpretation of what constitutes an immunity guaranteed by the Federal Constitution. They are Tullock v. Mulvane, 184 U. S. 497, and Bailey v. Alabama, 211 U. S. 452. The first involved the constitutionality of a decree of a state court which had given to a defendant the attorney's fees, in addition to damages for losses incurred by the unlawful imposition of an injunction issued by the circuit court. The question raised was whether there was a federal question involved such as would give jurisdiction to the federal court. The court, speaking through Justice White, said that there was, but Justice Harlan said there was not.

The following quotation will give in a general way the contention of the court: " To hold the contrary, as we have previously pointed out, would be but to declare, that although the power conferred by Congress upon this court to adopt equity rules in controlling, nevertheless the interpretations of the rules and limitations which arise from a proper construction of them, as expounded by this court and enunciated in its decisions, are without avail. And this yet further points out the fallacy involved in the contention that the lower court, in passing upon the issues, decided merely a question of general law involving no Federal controversy. Now it is at once conceded that the decision by a state court of a question of local or general law involving no Federal element does not as a matter of course present a Federal question. But, where, on the contrary, a Federal element is specially averred and essentially involved, the duty of this court to apply to such Federal question its own conceptions of the general law we think is incontrovertible."

The decision of the court amounted to this : If there arose a dispute involving the application of law in which a federal right was averred, even though there was no constitutional point involved, and though there was no federal statute covering the case and the matter controlled was one of private relations within the State, yet what the federal court had decided as having had bearing on this point should be given precedence over state law and decisions. As Justice Harlan showed, this was an inadmissible extension of federal authority.

He said : " The claim is that the rules and decisions of the Supreme Court of the United States have the force of legislative declarations ; that they enter into, and become a part of, the contract of sureties, who can only be held liable for such consequences as are the direct result of the breach and were within their contemplation at the time the bond was executed. No statute, however, prescribed the conditions of the bond nor limited the extent of liability thereon. It is true that it was within the general equitable power of the Federal court to prescribe the conditions upon which the injunction should issue. . . . Being an independent contract, actionable in any state court where service upon the sureties can be obtained, the interpretation of the former applies. . . . They knew that the obligation was enforceable in the courts of the state of which the plaintiff and defendants were all residents, and that the highest court of that state had consistently held that counsel fees were recoverable on an injunction bond. That the bond was given in a Federal court, where a different rule of interpretation obtains, has not been deemed to affect the state court in determining the liability upon such bonds when suit was brought thereon. . . .

" Suppose this court had not, prior to the trial of this case, expressed any opinion upon that question of general law. Could it then have been contended that the judgment complained of denied any Federal immunity? If not, then the Federal immunity now claimed arises entirely from the failure of the state court to take the same view of a question of general law which this court took in prior cases between other parties. There has been a wide difference of opinion between this court and some of the state courts upon questions of general law. But it has never been supposed that anyone has such a vested interest in the views of this court upon questions of general law that he may complain of the refusal of a state court to accept those views as denying him an 'immunity' existing or belonging to him in virtue of an 'authority exercised under the United States.'"

From a study of this decision it is very difficult to ascertain exactly what federal immunity the judge was defending. He was very positive in asserting that on the very face of the case a federal immunity was involved, but he was obscure in indicating exactly what that immunity was. The more clearly, however, the matter in dispute is brought into the foreground, the more certain it is that there was in fact no federal immunity. Justice Harlan showed that there had been many cases decided to the contrary, and that even the decisions cited by the court do not, if properly interpreted, give precedent for the present decree.

This case illustrates how far at times the court will go in order to discover a federal question. The next case for discussion shows how hard it is, at other times, for the court to see a federal question when it would seem to be very evident. Justice Harlan, of course, dissented from the latter also,—Bailey v. Alabama, 211 U. S. 452. The case came from the supreme court of Alabama, to review a decision denying relief by habeas corpus. The decision was rendered by Justice Holmes, and may be summarized as follows: The plaintiff in error was committed for detention on a charge of having obtained fifteen dollars with the intent to defraud his employer. The contention was that a colored man had by a statute of Alabama been deprived of his liberty without due process of law, and had been subjected to involuntary servitude.

The nature of the statute in question was this: If any one borrowed money in advance on a written contract for labor, a fine of double the amount borrowed was to be imposed upon the borrower if he refused to perform the work which he had agreed to perform. Half of the amount of the fine went to the State, and the other half went to the employer as a repayment of the amount lost. The following was the contested stipulation in the statute: "And the refusal of any person who enters into such contract to perform such act or service or to cultivate such lands, or refund such money, or pay for such property, without just cause, shall be prima facie evidence of the intent to injure his employer or landlord, or to defraud him."

The plea was set up that this statute made it possible, by the advancing of small amounts of money to persons in need, to prevent such persons from making free labor contracts. The fact that the non-performance of the work contracted for was to be taken on prima facie evidence of his intent to defraud made it impossible for the person, by working elsewhere, to pay the debt. Hence the plea was made that this was involuntary servitude.

The case was thrown out of court because of the way in which the plaintiff proceeded. The ruling was that because the plaintiff had sued out a writ of habeas corpus for discharge in advance of his trial in the lower state court, he had not taken the proper procedure to have his case determined by the Supreme Court. This was termed a "short cut" by the court, and because of this short cut the question asked could not be answered.

Such a grave injustice aroused Mr. Harlan. He recognized, however, that if this procedure had taken place in a lower federal court and the case had been appealed, the writ of habeas corpus would have been denied. But since this was a procedure in the state courts from the first, and since the supreme court of the State had overlooked this flaw in procedure, that fact once and for all settled the point of procedure in the lower state court. All that the Supreme Court was to decide, and had a right to decide, was the constitutionality of the statute. In other words, Justice Harlan contended that the Supreme Court exceeded its jurisdiction in passing upon the procedure in state courts, particularly when the supreme court of the State from which the case came had not questioned it.

"If the accused," he said, "in advance of his trial, had sought a discharge on a writ of *habeas corpus* sued out from *a circuit court of the United States,* that might have been deemed a 'short cut.' For it is well established that, 'in the light of the relations existing under our system of government between the judicial tribunals of the Union and of the states, and in recognition of the fact that the public good requires that those relations be not disturbed by unnecessary conflict between courts equally bound to guard and protect rights secured by the Constitution,' the courts of the United States will not, except in certain cases of urgency, and in advance of his trial, discharge, upon *habeas corpus,* one who is alleged to be held in custody by the state, in violation of the Constitution or the laws of the United States. . . . But whether the accused, in seeking his discharge by the state court, adopted a mode of procedure authorized by the local law, was for the Alabama courts, not for this court, to determine. The state court recognized the proceeding by *habeas corpus* to be in accordance with the local law; for the supreme court of Alabama, without even intimating that the accused took a 'short cut,' or pursued the wrong method to obtain his discharge, entertained his appeal and passed upon the constitutionality of the statute under which he was held in custody."

Without going further into this subject, it is readily seen, from these two cases, if the court wishes to see a federal question, how little excuse is necessary to find one, but if the court wishes to find otherwise, how much it takes to make the court pass upon the constitutionality of a question. With Justice Harlan it was not so. With him, if there was a federal question to be decided, it was the court's duty to pass upon it. If, on the other hand, there was none, he did not think it the duty of the court to manufacture one.

Equity Competence.—The case of Thompson v. Allen County, 115 U. S. 550, is an interesting illustration of Justice Harlan's desire to have the United States circuit court enforce its decree. Here was involved the issue by a county, in due legal form, of bonds as subscription to stock in a railroad company. The county court had been empowered by the State to appoint a tax collector to collect the tax levy to meet the interest on the coupons as it came due. The whole county was opposed to this tax levy, and practically everybody refused to pay. No one could be found by the county court who would undertake the duty of collecting taxes to meet the obligations which the county clearly owed. The circuit court issued a mandamus directed to the county court to have the taxes collected to meet the debt of the county. When the reply came that no one could be found to collect the taxes, suit was instituted to force the tax payers individually to pay the taxes in court for the purpose of meeting the interest due on the bonds. The circuit court held that the collection of taxes was not a judicial function, and upon this point the case was sustained by the Supreme Court.

The language of the court on this point is as follows: "No such power has ever yet been exercised by a court of chancery. The appointment of its officer to collect taxes levied by order of a common-law court is as much without authority as to appoint the same officer to levy and collect the tax. They are parts of the same proceeding, and relate to the same matter. If the common-law court can compel the *assessment* of a tax, it is quite as competent to enforce its *collection* as a court of chancery. Having jurisdiction to compel the assessment, there is no reason why it should stop short, if any further judicial power exists under the law, and turn the case over to a court of equity. The sheriff or marshal is as well qualified to collect the tax as a receiver appointed by the court of chancery."

Justice Harlan differed from the court both as to the collection of this tax being an assumption by the court of an executive function, and as to the ability of the circuit court to put into effect its mandamus by collecting the tax itself.

After citing several cases to show that such had not before been necessarily deemed an assumption of an inappropriate function, he said: "The bill does not ask the court to usurp the function of *levying* the taxes. That duty has been performed by the only tribunal authorized to do it, viz.: the County Court of Allen County. Nothing remains to be done, except to collect from individuals specific sums of money which they are under legal obligations to pay. The collection of these sums will not interfere with any discretion with which the Allen County Court is invested by law; for, by its own order, made in conformity with the law of the State, and by judgment in the *mandamus* proceedings, the sums due from the individual defendants, and from other taxpayers, have been set apart for the payment of Thompson's judgments. Those sums, when thus collected cannot be otherwise used. As the county court cannot find any one who will accept the office of special collector, and as the parties agree that there is no mode of collecting the sums set apart in the hands of the individual defendants and other tax payers, for the payment of Thompson, I am unable to perceive why the circuit court sitting in equity, may not cause these sums to be applied in satisfaction of its judgments at law. . . . With money in their hands, equitably belonging to the judgment creditor, they walk out of the court whose judgments remain unsatisfied, announcing in effect, that they will hold negotiations only with a ' special collector' who has no existence.

" That the court below, sitting in equity—after it has given a judgment at law for money, and after a return of *nulla bona* against the debtor—may not lay hold of moneys, set apart, *by the act of the debtor,* in the hands of individuals *exclusively for the payment of that judgment,* and which money, the parties agree, cannot be otherwise reached than by being brought into that court under its orders, is a confession of helplessness on the part of the courts of the United States that I am unwilling to make."

Amount in Dispute.—The question of the amount in dispute necessary for the Supreme Court to review decisions below has given rise to some very interesting discussions. The disputes, however, have not centered so much around the amount itself as around the constitutional points involved. Two cases illustrate this assertion, Linford v. Ellison, 155 U. S. 503, and Giles v. Harris, 189 U. S. 475.

The case of Linford v. Ellison involved the validity of an ordinance of the city of Kaysville, Utah. This ordinance levied a tax on land which, though incorporated within the city, was so far from the settled portions as not to be benefited by incorporation. A person having refused to pay the assessment made upon him, the tax collector levied and sold a wagon, to obtain the amount of fifty dollars to satisfy the assessment. The contention was made that inasmuch as the tax was levied upon one who received no benefit from the city, such a tax took property without due process of law.

The Supreme Court decided, among other things, that since the city had acted within authority granted by Congress in establishment of the territory of Utah, and since the constitutionality of no statute of Congress was involved, and since the damages did not amount to $5000, the decision of the territorial court would stand. The language of the court on this point is as follows: "It is thus seen that the decision of the supreme court of the territory involved the construction of the organic law and the scope of the authority to 'legislate conferred upon the territorial legislature; but that the validity of that authority and of the statute was not drawn in question. In order to give us jurisdiction of this appeal, the matter in dispute exclusive of costs must have exceeded the sum of $5,000, or else, without regard to the sum or value in dispute, the validity of a patent or copyright must have been involved, or the validity of a treaty or statute of or an authority exercised under the United States have been drawn in question."

Justice Harlan thought that the question should have been answered regardless of the amount in dispute. The question had been asked whether property had been taken without due process of law, and it was for the court to answer it. "We have jurisdiction to review the judgment or decree of the supreme court of a territory, without regard to the sum or value in dispute in any case in which is 'drawn in question the validity of . . . an authority exercised under the United States.'" Since "the validity of the authority given by the territorial legislature, acting under the United States, to tax agricultural lands like those belonging to the plaintiff, was directly drawn in question and was passed upon by the court of original jurisdiction," the question should have been answered.

In concluding, he said: "It seems to me that if a case in a territorial court turns upon the validity of an act which is authorized by a statute of the territorial legislature deriving its existence and powers from the United States, and if that statute is itself drawn in question as being repugnant to the Constitution of the United States, then we have a case in which is ' drawn in question the validity of . . . an authority exercised under the United States.' "

It may appear that this case involves primarily the construction of a statute, but underneath can be seen Justice Harlan's desire that the court shall determine the point of due process of law, and the desire to extend the jurisdiction of the Supreme Court as far as possible to acts of subordinate authorities in territories.

It has been seen how, in Bailey v. Alabama, Justice Holmes, by calling the procedure undergone by the plaintiff a short cut, denied to the colored man rights supposed to be secured to him under the Constitution of the United States. In Giles v. Harris occurs a similar situation. In this case, however, the court assumed jurisdiction and considered the merits of the case, but did not pass upon the constitutional point involved.

The case involved the provisions in the constitution of Alabama which had been so applied as to deny to the negroes the right to vote. The case was brought into the circuit court of the United States, and was dismissed for want of jurisdiction. Hence an appeal was taken to the Supreme Court. The dismissal from the circuit court was on the ground that damages were averred to be not two thousand dollars.

The Supreme Court admitted that the circuit court did not have jurisdiction as the record read, but rather than remand for a revision of the record, the court waived the pecuniary considerations and proceeded to decide the merits of the case. It decided that equity could not give relief, for the plaintiffs would have been forced by the court to be registered under a statute which they themselves said was unconstitutional. In the second place, it said that if the whole of the white population of Alabama desired to deprive the colored men of their votes, a decision to the contrary would not remedy the situation. But the court did not answer the question of the constitutionality of the provisions of the Alabama constitution, one of the express averments of the case.

Justice Harlan differed from the court because it discussed the merits of the case at all. He held that since the case was not properly before the circuit court in that the record did not show the averment of damages amounting to two thousand dollars, the question of damages could not rightly be waived by the Supreme Court and the case decided upon its merits. In that connection he said: " It seems to me that this question as to the value of the matter in dispute was sufficiently raised in the circuit court; for the demurrer to the bill was, in part, on the ground that the facts stated did not make a case ' within the jurisdiction of the court.' But, passing that view, I come to a more serious matter. In cases of which a circuit court may take original cognizance, the value of the matter in dispute—which is mentioned in the statute in advance of any reference to the nature of the subject of the action—is as essential to jurisdiction as is the nature of the subject of such dispute. And yet the court says that an objection that the record from the circuit court does not show an allegation as to value is unavailing here, even if such allegation ought to have been made. That is a new, and I take leave to say, a startling doctrine. Must not this court, upon its own motion, decline to pass upon—indeed has this court, strictly speaking, jurisdiction to consider and determine—the merits of a case coming from the circuit court, unless it *affirmatively* appears *from the record* that the case is one of which that court could take cognizance? Is not a suit presumably without the jurisdiction of a circuit court, unless the record shows it to be one of which that court may take cognizance? Is it of any consequence that the parties did not raise the question in the circuit court? If the record shows nothing more than that the case arises under the Constitution and laws of the United States, and if it does not affirmatively appear in some appropriate way, that the value of the matter in dispute is up to the required amount, has this court jurisdiction to consider and determine the merits of the case?"

In concluding he said: "My views may be summed up as follows: 1. This case is embraced by that clause of the act of 1887–88 which provides that the circuit court shall have original cognizance 'of all suits of a civil nature . . . where the matter in dispute exceeds, exclusive of interest and costs, the sum of $2,000, and arising under the constitution or laws of the United States.' 2. That the sum or value of the matter in dispute in such cases is jurisdictional under the statute. 3. That, as it did not appear from the record, in any way, that the matter in dispute exceeded in value the jurisdictional amount, the circuit court could not take cognizance or dispose of it on its merits. 4. That least of all does this court have jurisdiction to determine the merits of this case. 5. That when a case comes here upon a certificate as to the jurisdiction of a circuit court, this court may not forbear to decide that question, and determine the merits of the case upon a record which does not show jurisdiction in the circuit court." He added, however, "that it is competent for the court to give relief in such cases as this."

There is one characteristic in all of Justice Harlan's dissents on the ground of the jurisdiction of courts, namely, the desire to see justice done to the individual. If a person had been wronged in one court, and there was constitutional reason for having the case taken into another court and there dealing out justice to the individual, he was unwilling that the letter of the law should stand in the way. These cases well refute the accusation that has often been made against him that he stood for the letter rather than the spirit of the law.

CHAPTER VII

MISCELLANEOUS TOPICS

Bearing of the Fourteenth Amendment upon the First Eight Amendments.—Justice Harlan held, with regard to the fourteenth amendment, a doctrine which few seem to have supported. According to him, the provisions of the fourteenth amendment made the first eight amendments limitations upon the States as well as upon the United States. Since by the fourteenth amendment no State could abridge the privileges and immunities of citizens of the United States, no State could deny anything guaranteed in the first eight. These provisions had previously been considered privileges and immunities as opposed to the power of the national government. Since, therefore, the fourteenth amendment forbade the abridgment by the States of the privileges and immunities of citizens of the United States, it forbade the abridgment by them of those secured to the citizens by the first eight amendments.

In O'Neil v. State of Vermont, 144 U. S. 323, Justice Harlan, dissenting, expressed the following sentiment: " I fully concur with *Mr. Justice Field,* that since the adoption of the 14th Amendment, no one of the fundamental rights of life, liberty, or property, recognized and guaranteed by the Constitution of the United States, can be denied or abridged by a State in respect to any person within its jurisdiction. These rights are, principally, enumerated in the earlier amendments of the Constitution. They were deemed so vital to the safety and security of the people, that the absence from the Constitution, adopted by the convention of 1787, of express guarantees of them, came very near defeating the acceptance of that instrument by the requisite number of states. The Constitution was ratified in the belief, and only because of the belief, encouraged by its leading advocates, that, immediately upon the organization of the Government of the Union, articles of amendment would be submitted to the people, recognizing those essential rights of life, liberty, and property, which inhered in Anglo-Saxon freedom, and which our ancestors brought with them from the mother country."

In Maxwell v. Dow, 176 U. S. 581, Justice Harlan spoke even more vehemently for this principle. A man had been tried, convicted of robbery, and sentenced to eighteen years' imprisonment, by a jury of eight persons. The case was taken by writ of error from the supreme court of the State of Utah on the plea that the section of the constitution of that State which allowed trial by jury of less than twelve, was unconstitutional in that it deprived citizens of the United States of privileges and immunities secured to them by the Constitution of the United States.

The court, speaking through Justice Peckham, denied this claim. The main precedent cited was that established in the Slaughter House Cases, 16 Wall. 36, where it was developed " that there was a citizenship of the United States and a citizenship of the states, which were distinct from each other, depending upon different characteristics and circumstances in the individual; that it was only privileges and immunities of citizens of the United States that were placed by the amendment under the protection of the Federal Constitution, and that the privileges and immunities of a citizen of a state, whatever they might be, were not intended to have any additional protection by the paragraph in question, but they must rest for their security and protection where they have heretofore rested."

Justice Harlan, however, dissenting, said: " It does not solve the question before us to say that the first ten Amendments had a reference only to the powers of the national government, and not to the powers of the states. For, if, prior to the adoption of the Fourteenth Amendment, it was one of the privileges or immunities of citizens of the United

States that they should not be tried for crime in any court organized or existing under national authority except by a jury composed of twelve persons, how can it be that a citizen of the United States may be now tried in a state court for crime, particularly for an infamous crime, by eight jurors, when the Amendment expressly declares that 'no state shall make or enforce any law which shall abridge the privileges or immunities of citizens of the United States'? . . .

"If the court had not ruled otherwise, I should have thought it indisputable that when by the Fourteenth Amendment it was declared that no state should make or enforce any law abridging the privileges or immunities of citizens of the United States, nor deprive any person of life, liberty, or property without due process of law, the People of the United States put upon the states the same restrictions that had been imposed upon the national government in respect, as well of the privileges, and immunities of citizens of the United States, as of the protection of the fundamental rights of life, liberty, and property.

" The decision to-day rendered is very far-reaching in its consequences. I take it no one doubts that the great men who laid the foundations of our government regarded the preservation of the privileges and immunities specified in the first ten Amendments as vital to the personal security of American citizens. To say of any people that they do not enjoy those privileges and immunities is to say that they do not enjoy real freedom. . . .

"But, if I do not wholly misapprehend the scope and legal effect of the present decision, the Constitution of the United States does not stand in the way of any state striking down guaranties of life and liberty that English-speaking people have for centuries regarded as vital to personal security, and which the men of the revolutionary period universally claimed as the birthright of freemen."

It is seen from the above that Justice Harlan's doctrine rested on a basis deeper than mere logic. The principles stated in the first ten amendments were to him sacred elements of liberty, and he naturally opposed any decision that gave to the States a constitutional right to abridge those principles. He was not willing that the States individually should be left to determine whether their citizens had been deprived of any of the fundamental rights of freedom.

In Patterson v. Colorado, ex rel. Atty. Gen., 205 U. S. 454, Justice Harlan again asserted this doctrine in the following words: " I go further and hold that the privilege of free speech and of a free press, belonging to every citizen of the United States, constitute essential parts of every man's liberty, and are protected against violation by that clause of the 14th Amendment forbidding a state to deprive any person of his liberty without due process of law. It is, I think, impossible to conceive of liberty, as secured by the Constitution against hostile action, whether by the nation or by the states, which does not embrace the right to enjoy free speech and the right to have a free press."

In Twining v. New Jersey, 211 U. S. 78, as late as the year 1908, Justice Harlan asserted the same doctrine: "At the close of the late Civil War, which had seriously disturbed the foundations of our governmental system, the question arose whether provision should not be made by constitutional Amendments to secure against attack by the *states*, the rights, privileges, and immunities which, by the original Amendments, had been placed beyond the power of the United States or any Federal agency to impair or destroy. Those rights, privileges, and immunities had not then, in terms, been guarded by the national Constitution against impairment or destruction by the states, although, before the adoption of the 14th Amendment, every state, without, perhaps, an exception, had, in some form, recognized, as part of its fundamental law, most, if not all, the rights and immunities mentioned in the original Amendments, among them immunity from self-incrimination."

Direct Taxation.—It will be interesting from the standpoint of history to make a short study of Justice Harlan's dissent in the case of Pollock v. Farmers' Loan and Trust Co., 157 U. S. 429, 158 U. S. 601, wherein he differed from the court as to the meaning of direct taxation. As is well known, the court has not been uniform in its decisions as to what constitutes direct taxation. At first it was thought that only capitation taxes and taxes on real estate were direct taxes, but in the case under consideration it was declared that taxes on income from real estate and from personal property are direct taxes.

As the case was tried when, owing to the sickness of one of the justices, there were only eight sitting, and as the judges were equally divided on various aspects of the case, a rehearing was granted. At the first hearing the court ruled that the law in question, so far as it levied a tax on the rents or income of real estate, was in violation of the Constitution and invalid. But the judges were divided equally on the following points: " 1. Whether the void provision [as to rents and income from real estate] invalidates the whole act? 2. Whether as to the income from personal property as such, the act is unconstitutional, as laying direct taxes? 3. Whether any part of the tax, if not considered as a direct tax, is invalid for want of uniformity on either of the grounds suggested?" Upon the rehearing the case was decided affirmatively on each of the above points. Justice Harlan dissented from the whole decision of the court. His full doctrine was brought out in his dissent in the final hearing of the case.

His first condemnation of the decision was based upon the court's disloyalty to the doctrine of stare decisis. After recalling that there had been much difference of opinion in the constitutional convention as to exactly what constituted a direct tax, he showed that it had been decided in Hylton v. United States, 3 Dall. 171, that nothing except taxes upon real estate and capitation taxes constitutes direct taxes, and therefore that in asserting that taxation upon income from real estate or personal property was direct taxation the court departed from the accepted doctrine. Many other cases were cited to develop this argument. He said: "It seems to me that the court has not given to the maxim of *stare decisis* the full effect to which it is entitled. While obedience to that maxim is not expressly enjoined by the Constitution, the principle that decisions, resting upon a particular interpretation of that instrument, should not be lightly disregarded where such interpretation has been long accepted and acted upon by other branches of the government and by the public, underlies our American jurisprudence. . . . While, in a large sense, constitutional questions may not be considered as finally settled, unless settled rightly, it is certain that a departure by this court from a settled course of decisions on grave constitutional questions, under which vast transactions have occurred, and under which the government has been administered during great crises, will shake public confidence in the stability of the law."

"I have a deep, abiding conviction," he continued, "which my sense of duty compels me to express, that it is not possible for this court to have rendered any judgment more to be regretted than the one just rendered. . . . In my judgment a tax on *income* derived from real property ought not to be, and until now has never been, regarded by any court as a direct tax on such property within the meaning of the Constitution. . . . And, in view of former adjudications, beginning with the *Hylton case* and ending with the *Springer case,* a decision now that a tax on income from real property can be laid and collected only by apportioning the same among the states, on the basis of numbers, may, not improperly, be regarded as a judicial revolution, that may sow the seeds of hate and distrust among the people of different sections of our common country."

Though the above quotation might seem to indicate that Justice Harlan did not look at the economic meaning of a direct tax, the following will show that he was not unaware of this consideration: "In determining whether a tax on income from rents is a direct tax, within the meaning of the

Constitution, the inquiry is not whether it may in some way indirectly affect the land or the landowner, but whether it is a *direct* tax *on the thing taxed, the land*. The circumstance that such a tax may possibly have the effect to diminish the value of the use of the land is neither decisive of the question nor important. While a tax *on the land* itself, whether at a fixed rate applicable to all lands without regard to their value, or by the acre or according to their market value, might be deemed a direct tax within the meaning of the Constitution as interpreted in the *Hylton case,* a duty on rents is a duty on something distinct and entirely separate from, although issuing out of, the land."

In the next place, Justice Harlan proceeded to show how much more unreasonable was the decision that income from tangible personal property should not be subject to a tax by the national government under a rule of uniformity than was the decision regarding income from real estate. "When direct taxes are restricted to capitation taxes and taxes on land, taxation, in either form, is limited to subjects always found wherever population is found, and which cannot be consumed or destroyed. They are subjects which can always be seen and inspected by the assessor, and have immediate connection with the country and its soil throughout its entire limits. Not so with personal property."

Furthermore, he upbraided the court for this decision because of the practical results to be expected from it regardless of former adjudications. "Why do I say that the decision just rendered impairs or menaces the national authority? The reason is so apparent that it need only be stated. In its practical operation this decision withdraws from national taxation not only all incomes derived from real estate, but tangible personal property, '*invested* personal property, bonds, stocks, investments of all kinds,' and the income that may be derived from such property. This results from the fact that by the decision of the court, all such personal property and all incomes from real estate and personal property, are placed beyond national taxation otherwise than by *apportionment* among the states *on the basis* simply *of population.* No such apportionment can possibly be made without doing gross injustice to the many for the benefit of the favored few in particular states. Any attempt upon the part of Congress to apportion among the states, upon the basis simply of their population, taxation of personal property or of incomes, would tend to arouse such indignation among the freemen of America that it would never be repeated. When, therefore, this court adjudges, as it does now adjudge, that Congress cannot impose a duty or tax upon personal property, or upon income arising either from rents of real estate or from personal property, 'including invested personal property, bonds, stocks, and investments of all kinds,' except by apportioning the sum to be so raised among the states according to population, it *practically* decides that, *without an amendment of the Constitution*—two thirds of both Houses of Congress and three fourths of the states concurring—such property and incomes can never be made to contribute to the support of the national government."

In closing he said: "The practical effect of the decision to-day is to give to certain kinds of property a position of favoritism and advantage inconsistent with the fundamental principles of our social organization, and to invest them with power and influence that may be perilous to that portion of the American people upon whom rests the larger part of the burdens of government, and who ought not to be subjected to the dominion of aggregated wealth any more than the property of the country should be at the mercy of the lawless."

The question as to what is in fact a direct tax is impossible of solution. The court had already hit upon two things that were as nearly direct taxes as anything could be, and there the matter should have rested. The effect of the decision was to make necessáry an amendment to the Constitution of the United States.

Ex Post Facto Laws.—The case of Hawker v. New York,

170 U. S. 189, shows what Justice Harlan conceived to be an ex post facto law. The case arose because of the denial to a physician, by a statute of the State of New York, of the right to practice medicine. The doctor had been convicted of the crime of abortion and sentenced to a term of ten years in the penitentiary. He had served his term and was again engaged in practice when the State passed a statute providing that no one who had been convicted of felony should practice medicine. The doctor was arrested and was fined two hundred and fifty dollars for treating a patient, and this case was taken by way of appeal to the Supreme Court of the United States upon the plea that the later statute was an ex post facto law.

The court held that law valid, and said: " The state is not seeking to further punish a criminal, but only to protect its citizens from physicians of bad character. The vital matter is not the conviction, but the violation, of law. The former is merely the prescribed evidence of the latter. Suppose the statute had contained only a clause declaring that no one should be permitted to act as a physician who had violated the criminal laws of the state, leaving the question of the violation to be determined according to the ordinary rules of evidence, would it not seem strange to hold that that which conclusively established the fact effectually relieved from the consequences of such violation?"

To Justice Harlan this argument was unconvincing. His claim was that if the previous law had stipulated as a part of the punishment of felonies that a physician should not thereafter practice medicine, the denial of the privilege to Hawker would not have been ex post facto. But since he had suffered the penalty imposed by the State for the crime committed, any additional punishment inflicted for the same offence would be ex post facto. " If the statute in force when the offense of abortion was committed had provided that, *in addition* to imprisonment in the penitentiary, the accused, if convicted, should not thereafter practice medicine, no one, I take it, would doubt that such prohibition was a part of the *punishment* prescribed for the offense. And yet it would seem to be the necessary result of the opinion of the court in the present case, that a statute passed after the commission of the offense of 1877 and which by its own force, made it a crime for defendant *to continue* in the practice of medicine, is not an addition to the punishment inflicted upon him in 1878. I cannot assent to this view. It is, I think, inconsistent with the provision of the Constitution of the United States declaring that no State shall pass any *ex post facto* law."

Justice Harlan also urged the fact that the offender might have become a different sort of man after serving in prison and therefore be well suited to practice medicine. But that point seems to be wide of the mark. It has an important ethical consideration, but could have no bearing upon an ex post facto law as such, for the State would have been denying this opportunity of reform if it had been a part of the punishment of the crime from the beginning that a physician guilty of felony should not again practice medicine.

But it might be argued that the first contention was well founded. It depends upon whether the law is considered simply as a provision to insure suitable characters for the practice of medicine. That is a legitimate police measure, within the power of the State. If the law be looked upon merely as instituting a punishment, it must be admitted that Justice Harlan was contending correctly that the law was an ex post facto law, for the statute in question not only operated as a punishment for crime after it had been committed, but also after the man had been punished to the full extent of the law as it existed at the time of the commission of the crime.

Copyrights.—The Constitution of the United States gives Congress the power to pass laws promoting science and useful arts by means of patents and copyrights. Under the statutes regulating copyrights a very amusing case came up from the United States circuit court for the district of

Kentucky.[1] This court had decided that certain copies of pictures of dancing girls from advertisements of the Wallace circus were not protected by the laws regulating the production of useful arts. The case having been appealed to the Supreme Court, the decision of the lower court was reversed.

The following quotation from the decision, rendered by Justice Holmes, will show the ground of the reversal: "It would be a dangerous undertaking for persons trained only to the law to constitute themselves final judges of the worth of pictorial illustrations, outside of the narrowest and most obvious limits. At the one extreme, some works of genius would be sure to miss appreciation. Their very novelty would make them repulsive until the public had learned the new language in which their author spoke. It may be more than doubted, for instance, whether the etchings of Goya or the paintings of Manet would have been sure of protection when seen for the first time. At the other end, copyrights would be denied to pictures which appealed to a public less educated than the judge. Yet if they command the interest of any public, they have a commercial value—and it would be bold to say that they have not an aesthetic and educational value—and the taste of any public is not to be treated with contempt. It is an ultimate fact for the moment, whatever may be our hope for a change. That these pictures had their worth and their success is sufficiently shown by the desire to reproduce them without regard to the plaintiff's right."

These words sound almost sublime, but it must be admitted that they become ludicrous when used in connection with a bill-board advertising circus dancing girls. And that is the substance of Justice Harlan's dissent. "The clause of the Constitution giving Congress the power to promote the progress of science and useful arts, by securing for limited terms to authors and inventors the exclusive use of their respective work and discoveries, does not, as I think, embrace a mere advertisement of a circus."

---

[1] Bleistein v. Donaldson Lith. Co., 188 U. S. 239.

Self-Incrimination.—In Twining v. New Jersey, 211 U. S. 78, the court held that freedom from self-incrimination is not one of those privileges secured to citizens by the due process of law clause of the fourteenth amendment. In dissenting Justice Harlan criticized the court's refusal to determine whether self-incriminatory evidence had been demanded. A question of so much import, he said, should not be decided unless it is necessary in order to decide the case: "As a reason why it takes up first the question of the power of a state, so far as the Federal Constitution is concerned, to compel self-incrimination, the court says that if the right here asserted is not a Federal right that is an end of the case, and it must not go further. It would, I submit, have been more appropriate to say that, if no ground whatever existed, under the facts disclosed by the record, to contend that a Federal right had been violated, this court would be without authority to go further and express its opinion on an abstract question relating to the powers of the states under the constitution."

But Justice Harlan further contended that if the court had found that the right had been violated it should have pronounced the act of the State unconstitutional, because, in the first place, he believed that the privileges and immunities of citizens of the United States which were secured against state action by the fourteenth amendment included also those enumerated in the first eight; and in the second place, even if this were not true, a proper interpretation of the phrase "due process of law" includes freedom from self-incrimination. In this connection he said: "In my judgment, immunity from self-incrimination is protected against hostile state action, not only by that clause in the 14th Amendment declaring that 'no state shall make or enforce any law which shall abridge the privileges or immunities of citizens of the United States,' but by the clause, in the same Amendment, 'nor shall any state deprive any person of life, liberty, or property, without due process of law.' No argument is needed to support the proposition that, whether manifested by statute or by the final judgment of a court, state action, if liable to the objection that it abridges the privileges or immunities of national citizenship, must also be regarded as wanting in the due process of law enjoined by the 14th Amendment, when such state action substantially affects life, liberty, or property."

The Insular Cases.—Justice Harlan did not render a separate dissenting opinion in the earlier of the Insular cases. His concurrence in the dissent by Chief Justice Fuller in Downes v. Bidwell, 182 U. S. 244, however, showed that he was opposed to the differentiation made by the court, namely, that which placed the power of Congress over the insular possessions in certain respects above the Constitution of the United States. The case of Hawaii v. Mankichi, 190 U. S. 197, contains the substance of his whole doctrine regarding the relation of the United States to the newly acquired territory.

The question at issue in Hawaii v. Mankichi was whether the Constitution in full force had been extended to the Hawaiian Islands by the joint resolution of Congress annexing them. The opinion of the court in this case was very hotly opposed by Justice Harlan, Chief Justice Fuller, and Justice Peckham. The majority opinion was rendered by Justice Brown, and concurring opinions were submitted by Justices White and McKenna. Thus it is seen that the court was sharply divided.

The case came up for review from the United States district court for Hawaii, which had discharged on habeas corpus a man convicted of manslaughter because he had been convicted by a verdict of only nine of the twelve jurors. The decision of the lower court was that such conviction was not in accordance with the guarantee by the Constitution of the United States of trial by jury, in that according to the American law the jury must agree unanimously on their verdict. The laws of Hawaii allowed such a procedure, and thus was raised the question whether the Constitution of the United States extended with full force over the Hawaiian Islands after their annexation to this country.

The decision of the court in this case was based upon the idea that the intention and not the letter of the law is the law. "'A thing may be within the letter of a statute and not within its meaning, and within its meaning, though not within its letter. The intention of the lawmaker is the law.' . . . There are many reasons which induce us to hold that the act was not intended to interfere with the existing practice, when such interference would result in imperiling the peace and good order of the islands."

It is seen that the argument of the court was based upon the meaning of the resolution, that is, whether it intended to extend to the islands all of the privileges and rights secured by the Constitution. This question Justice Harlan said could not be raised. He contended that it is not for Congress to say whether the Constitution is to operate in territory which had been incorporated within the jurisdiction of the United States. If it is constitutional for Congress to admit territory by joint resolution, well and good, but there is where the power of Congress stops. Any attempt to allow in the territories acts which are unconstitutional must be void.

He said: "In my opinion, the Constitution of the United States became the supreme law of Hawaii immediately upon the acquisition by the United States of complete sovereignty over the Hawaiian Islands, and without any act of Congress formally extending the Constitution to those islands. It then, at least, became controlling, beyond the power of Congress to prevent. From the moment when the government of Hawaii accepted the joint resolution of 1898, by a formal transfer of its sovereignty to the United States— when the flag of Hawaii was taken down, by authority of Hawaii, and in its place was raised that of the United States —every human being in Hawaii, charged with the commission of crime there, could have rightly insisted that neither his life nor his liberty could be taken as a punishment for

crime, by any process, or as a result of any mode of procedure that was inconsistent with the Constitution of the
United States. Can it be that the Constitution of the United
States is the supreme law in the states of the Union, in the
organized territories of the United States, between the Atlantic and Pacific Oceans, and in the District of Columbia,
and yet was not, prior to the act of 1900, the supreme law
in the territories and among the people situated as were the
territory and people of Hawaii, and over which the United
States had acquired all rights of sovereignty of whatsoever
kind? A negative answer to this question, and a recognition of the principle that such an answer involves would
place Congress above the Constitution. . . .

"I am of opinion: 1. That when the annexation of Hawaii
was completed, the Constitution—without any declaration
to that effect by Congress, and without any power of Congress to prevent it—became the supreme law for that country, and, therefore, it forbade the trial and conviction of
the accused for murder otherwise than upon a presentment
or an indictment of a grand jury, and by the unanimous
verdict of a petit jury. 2. That if the legality of such trial
and conviction is to be tested alone by the Joint Resolution
of 1898, then the law is for the accused, because Congress,
by that Resolution, abrogated, or forbade the enforcement
of, any municipal law of Hawaii, so far as it authorized a
trial for an infamous crime otherwise than in the mode prescribed by the Constitution of the United States; and that
any other construction of the resolution is forbidden by its
clear, unambiguous words, and is to make, not to interpret,
the law."

One other quotation will be to the point: "I stand by the
doctrine that the Constitution is the supreme law in every
territory, as soon as it comes under the sovereign dominion
of the United States for purposes of civil administration,
and whose inhabitants are under its entire authority and
jurisdiction. I could not otherwise hold without conceding
the power of Congress, the creature of the Constitution, by

mere nonaction, to withhold vital constitutional guarantees from the inhabitants of a territory governed by the authority and only by the authority of the United States. Such a doctrine would admit of the exercise of absolute, arbitrary legislative power under a written Constitution full of restrictions upon Congress, and designed to limit the separate departments of government to the exercise of only expressly enumerated powers and such other powers as may be implied therefrom,—each department always acting in subordination to that instrument as the supreme law of the land. Indeed, it has been announced by some statesmen that the Constitution should be interpreted to mean, not what its words naturally, or usually, or even plainly, import, but what the apparent necessities of the hour, or the apparent majority of the people, at a particular time, demand at the hands of the judiciary. I cannot assent to any such view of the Constitution. Nor can I approve of the suggestion that the status of Hawaii and the powers of its local government are to be ' measured ' by the resolution of 1898, without reference to the Constitution. It is impossible for me to grasp the thought that that which is admittedly contrary to the supreme law can be sustained as valid."

These sentiments were reasserted in dissenting in the cases of Dorr v. United States, 195 U. S. 138, and Trono v. United States, 199 U. S. 521. Since, however, the views expressed in his opinions there were substantially the same as those expressed in the case of Hawaii v. Mankichi, they need not be discussed further.

Interstate Comity.—Though the question of interstate comity is a broad one, the points wherein Justice Harlan differed from the court have not been numerous. The case of Chambers v. Baltimore and Ohio R. Co., 207 U. S. 142, is the only one that needs to be considered. In this case was involved the right of a citizen of Pennsylvania, the widow of a fireman on the Baltimore and Ohio Railroad, who was also a citizen of Pennsylvania, to sue in an Ohio court. Suit had been brought in the lower court and dam-

ages amounting to $3000 had been allowed. But this deci-
sion had been reversed by the supreme court of the State of
Ohio, on the ground that the plaintiff could not sue in the
Ohio courts because of a statute of Ohio which prevented
it. Whereupon the case was appealed to the Supreme Court
of the United States upon the ground that the statute was
in violation of the clause of the federal Constitution which
provides that "the citizens of each State shall be entitled to
all privileges and immunities in the several States."

The court upheld the statute on the ground that it did not
make any discrimination against citizens of other States.
"The courts were open in such cases to plaintiffs who were
citizens of other states if the deceased was a citizen of
Ohio; they were closed to plaintiffs who were citizens of
Ohio if the deceased was a citizen of another state. So
far as the parties to the litigation are concerned, the state,
by its laws, made no discrimination based on citizenship,
and offered precisely the same privileges to citizens of other
states which it allowed to its own."

Justice Harlan differed from the court in that it presumed
to interpret the statute for itself instead of considering the
law as it stood under the interpretation of the state court.
The state court had expressly said that if the plaintiff had
been a citizen of the State of Ohio the damages would have
been held valid. "That there may be no mistake as to the
decision, I quote the official syllabus of the present case,
which, by the law of Ohio, is to be taken as indicating the
point actually in judgment: 'No action can be maintained
in the courts of this state upon a cause of action for wrong-
ful death occurring in another state, *except* where the person wrongfully killed was a *citizen of the state of Ohio.*' . . .

"In that view, if two persons, one a citizen of Ohio and
the other a citizen of Pennsylvania, travelling together on a
railroad in Pennsylvania, should be killed at the same moment and under precisely the same circumstances, in consequence of the negligence or default of the railroad company, the courts of Ohio are closed by its statute against

any suit for damages brought by the widow or the estate of the citizen of Pennsylvania against the railroad company, but will be open to suit by the widow or the estate of the deceased citizen of Ohio, although by the laws of the state where the death occurred the widow or estate of each decedent would have, in the latter state, a valid cause of action. . . .

"With entire respect for the views of others, I am constrained to say that in my opinion, so much of the local law, whether statutory or otherwise, as permits suits of this kind for damages where the deceased was not a citizen of Ohio, is unconstitutional."

Thus it is seen that Justice Harlan would have been more strict than the court was in its interpretation of the clause of the Constitution which secures interstate comity. There is also seen another instance of his desire to secure legal remedies to the individual.

Labor Legislation.—Under the head of labor legislation it is necessary to refer to some cases which are not primarily concerned with constitutional law. From Justice Harlan's dissents from these cases may be gathered a general impression of his attitude regarding the relation of the Constitution to labor reform.

The case of New England R. Co. v. Conroy, 175 U. S. 323, presents a very interesting dispute between Justice Harlan and the court as to the meaning of a fellow-servant. Justice Harlan contended that the conductor should have been looked upon as the representative of the railroad company on the trains, and that all of his subordinates were responsible to the company through him, when by pronouncing the conductor a fellow-servant with a brakeman the Court exempted the railroad company from damages which a jury had granted. "In my judgment," he said, "the conductor of a railroad train is the representative of the company in respect of its management, all the other employees on the train are his subordinates in matters involved in such management, and for injury received by any one of those subordinates during the management of the train by reason of the negligence of the conductor the railroad company should be held responsible."

Again, in Baltimore and Ohio Southwestern R. Co. v. Voigt, 176 U. S. 498, when the Supreme Court declared that an express messenger could not be termed a passenger, and hence could not receive damages for injuries sustained in a wreck, Justice Harlan dissented. He contended that such persons ought not to be excluded from that class of persons who could recover damages for injuries received while working on trains. He said: "I am of opinion that the present case is within the doctrines of *New York C. R. Co. v. Lockwood,* and that the judgment should be affirmed upon the broad ground that the defendant corporation could not, in any form, stipulate for exemption from responsibility for the negligence of its servants or employees in the course of its business, whereby injury comes to any person using its cars, with its consent for purposes of transportation. That the person transported is not technically a passenger and does not ride in a car ordinarily used for passengers is immaterial."

This natural sympathy for the employee or laborer, which was evidenced in the two cases just mentioned, came out in full force in his dissent from Lochner v. New York, 198 U. S. 45. Here the Supreme Court held invalid a law of New York which attempted to limit the hours of employment of bakers to ten hours a day. The court declared that such legislation was "an arbitrary interference with the freedom to contract guaranteed by the 14th Amendment which cannot be sustained as a valid exercise of the police power to protect the public health, safety, and morals, or general welfare." In a somewhat lengthy dissent from this case Justice Harlan undertook to prove by quotations from various sociological and medical authorities that the trade of a baker had a tendency to shorten the lives of those engaged in it.

He dissented again from the case of Howard v. Illinois Central R. Co., 207 U. S. 463, when the court declared unconstitutional the federal employers' liability act of June 11, 1906. While he did not think that this act could apply to intrastate commerce, he contended that it should have been declared effective for injuries which could be shown to have occurred in interstate commerce.

CHAPTER VIII

Judicial Legislation

It is particularly interesting to note the fact that the first and last dissenting opinions which Justice Harlan delivered were on the subject of judicial legislation. And there is no marked difference in the tone of these opinions, except that the first contained the firmness and positiveness of a middle-aged man, while the last contained the uneasiness and solicitude of an old man. In the first was a clear and definite respect for legislation as it read, in the last was a spirited condemnation of society for looking to the court to correct legislation. While the first was directed only to the court, the last was broader and contained a sting for any one who desired to extend the power of the court beyond its duly recognized judicial power. The first case was that of United States v. Clark, 96 U. S. 37, the last cases were the Standard Oil Company and American Tobacco Company decisions, 221 U. S. 1 and 106. Many times between these are found reassertions of the same sentiment.

Discussion of Cases.—The case of United States v. Clark will bear emphasis not only because it stands in direct relation to our subject, but also because it was Justice Harlan's first dissenting opinion. The case came up from the court of claims of the United States. A man named Clark, who was paymaster in the northern army during the Civil War, claimed that he had been robbed of the sum of $15,978.87. The questions at issue were whether Clark could be allowed to testify in his own behalf as to the amount stolen, and whether he was excluded from the court of claims anyway because he had waited too long to bring suit.

The first point made by the counsel for the United States, namely, that the plaintiff could not be allowed to testify in his own behalf, was easily overruled by asserting that though the claimant's testimony could not be accepted as valid testimony, " it may be proper as corroborative " of the alleged amount. The other contention on the part of the counsel for the government was as easily disposed of by asserting that the right of the claimant did not accrue until the accounting officers had held him liable for the sum lost. By this interpretation the suit was brought within the time allowed.

Justice Harlan approved of neither of these rulings. He thought that the judgment of the court of claims should have been reversed, with an order that the case be dismissed. Referring to the first point, he said: " In all ' Courts of the United States ' parties may testify, but in the *Court of Claims* no plaintiff can testify against the United States in support of his claim or right. So reads the statute; and it is, I submit, the duty of this court to obey it, leaving to Congress to make such changes in the rules of evidence in the Court of Claims as its views of public policy may suggest. It may be unfortunate for Clark if he be denied an opportunity to testify as to the amount of his loss; but, as said by Lord Campbell, *Ch. J.*, ' It is the duty of all courts of justice to take care, for the general good of the community, that hard cases do not make bad law.' " He said further: " With entire respect for the opinion of my brethren, I submit that the construction which the court places upon the Act of June 25, 1868, seems to fall very little short of judicial legislation."

He referred to the second point in the following words: " Clark, in order to obtain relief from responsibility on account of the alleged robbery, was required to present to the proper accounting officers a decree of the Court of Claims, directing that he should receive credit for the amount taken from him by robbery. It was not, therefore, a misuse of words for Congress to describe a demand for relief under the Act of 1866 as a ' claim.' If a ' claim,' it was clearly barred by the Act of 1863, unless it be true.as suggested in the opinion of the court that the claim did not accrue until the credit which Clark had given himself in his report of the robbery was rejected at the Treasury in 1871; but, unquestionably, his crediting himself with the amount taken from him by the robbery was an unauthorized act. The accounting officers could not, except in pursuance of a decree of the Court of Claims, lawfully allow such a credit; and their failure to promptly disallow it did not give Clark any additional right, nor deprive the Government of any right which it possessed. Neither his nor their action could suspend the running of the Statute of Limitations. His claim, therefore, accrued immediately upon the passage of the Act of May 9, 1866. Not having been asserted by suit within six years from that date, it was barred."

It has not been thought necessary to explain the meaning of the various acts referred to which established and laid down rules for the conduct of trials in the court of claims. It is sufficiently evident that the stipulation was made that the claim had to be set up within six years after it accrued, and that the court quibbled over what is meant by a claim in order to prevent that stipulation from debarring the suit. It is also evident that Justice Harlan thought that the quibble of the court was unjustified.

This case is typical as illustrating Justice Harlan's conception of the position which the court should occupy in our government. If any case could have arisen which would have called for the sacrifice of his conviction on this subject, this case certainly would have had that effect. He himself had been a commander in the northern army. Here was a paymaster of that army, from whom fifteen thousand dollars had been stolen, but so far as a proper interpretation of the law went, he had to lose that amount. If anything would have aroused Justice Harlan's sympathy this loss on the part of a fellow soldier should certainly have done so, and it doubtless did. But he recognized the necessity of having the court interpret the law for the general good of the nation. His conviction as to the integrity of the law was a higher conviction than that one unfortunate man should not suffer. The case, however, does not argue that he put the letter of the law above the spirit of it. Other cases where a possible interpretation would allow the individual to be benefited show the reverse as to his manner of approaching a decision. But since the letter and the spirit both in this case called for a different interpretation, he held that it should have been interpreted differently.

In following out the course of Justice Harlan's utterances on this matter, brief references only will be necessary in most cases. It was found that in the Civil Rights Cases, 109 U. S. 3, he thought that the court had no right to declare what was appropriate legislation for the enforcement of the thirteenth and fourteenth amendments. He said: "Under given circumstances, that which the court characterizes as corrective legislation might be deemed by Congress as appropriate legislation and entirely sufficient. Under other circumstances primary direct legislation may be required. But it is for Congress, not the judiciary, to say that legislation is appropriate; that is, best adapted to the end to be attained. The judiciary may not with safety to our institutions enter the domain of legislative discretion, and dictate the means which Congress shall employ in the exercise of its granted powers. That would be sheer usurpation of the functions of a co-ordinate department, which, if often repeated, would work a radical change in our system."

In Pollock v. Farmers' Loan and Trust Co., 158 U. S. 601, Justice Harlan spoke as follows: "It was said in argument that the passage of the statute imposing this income tax was an assault by the poor upon the rich, and by much eloquent speech this court has been urged to stand in the breach for the protection of the just rights of property against the advancing hosts of Socialism. With the policy of legislation of this character, the court has nothing to do. That is for the legislative branch of the government. It is for Congress to determine whether the necessities of the government are to be met, or the interests of the people subserved, by the taxation of incomes. With that determination, so far as it rests upon grounds of expediency or public policy, the courts can have no rightful concern. The safety and permanency of our institutions demand that each department of government shall keep within its legitimate sphere as defined by the supreme law of the land. We deal here only with questions of law."

In Robertson v. Baldwin, 165 U. S. 275, a similar utterance is found: "It will not do to say that by 'immemorial usage' seamen could be held in a condition of involuntary servitude, without having been convicted of crime. The people of the United States, by an amendment to their fundamental law, have solemnly decreed that 'except as a punishment for crime, whereof the party shall have been duly convicted,' involuntary servitude shall not exist in any form in this country. The adding of another exception by interpretation simply, and without amending the Constitution, is, I submit, judicial legislation. It is a very serious matter when a judicial tribunal, by the construction of an act of Congress, defeats the expressed will of the legislative branch of government. It is a still more serious matter when the clear reading of a constitutional provision relating to the liberty of a man is departed from in deference to what is called usage which has existed, for the most part, under monarchical and despotic governments."

As was seen in Hawaii v. Mankichi, 190 U. S. 197, Justice Harlan accused the court of so interpreting an act of Congress that it amounted to the passage by that body of an act which it could not constitutionally pass, and gave a meaning to it which Congress clearly did not intend that it should have. He said: "The opinion of the court contains observations to the effect that some persons, heretofore convicted of crime in the Hawaiian courts, will escape punishment if the joint resolution of 1898 is so interpreted as to make Congress mean what, it is conceded, the words 'contrary to the Constitution of the United States' naturally import. In the eye of the law that is of no consequence.

The cases cited by the court fall far short of sustaining the proposition that the court may reject the plain, obvious meaning of the words of the statute in order to remedy what it deems an omission by Congress. The consequences of a particular construction may be taken into account only when the words to be construed are ambiguous."

In the case of Houghton v. Payne, 194 U. S. 88, there is a characteristic dissent by Justice Harlan. Houghton, Mifflin and Company, publishers of the Riverside Literature Series, thought that they were treated wrongly in having these publications termed third-class matter, because, in spite of the fact that each volume was complete in itself, the volumes were issued periodically. For sixteen years the post-office department had interpreted the portion of the statute of Congress bearing on this point to mean that the Riverside Series were periodicals instead of books. Several attempts had been made to get Congress to amend the statute, but all had failed. Postmaster-General Payne, however, deliberately classed the Riverside Series as third-class matter, and the rate was changed accordingly. The publishers brought suit to have the action of Payne pronounced invalid. This the lower court refused to do, and upon appeal to the United States Supreme Court the decision below was sustained. The court reasoned as follows: " While it might well happen that by reason of the relative unimportance of the question when originally raised a too liberal construction might have been given to the word periodical, we cannot think that if this question had been raised for the first time after second class mail matter had obtained its present proportions, a like construction would have been given. Some considerations in connection with the revocation of these certificates may properly be accorded to the great expense occasioned by this interpretation, and the discrimination in favor of certain publishers and against others, to which allusion has already been made. We regard publications of the Riverside Literature Series as too clearly within the denomination of books to justify us in approving a classification of them as periodicals, notwithstanding the length of time such classification obtained."

Justice Harlan, with whom concurred the Chief Justice, thought that the court exceeded its power in this case and did what amounted to amending an act of Congress. His language on this point is as follows: " In our judgment, the appellants properly construe the statute. We think it obviously means just what the Department held it to mean for more than sixteen years. But the very utmost that the government can claim is that the statute in question is doubtful in meaning and scope. The rule in such a case is not to disturb the long continued practice of the Department in its execution of a statute, leaving to Congress to change it when public interests require that to be done. But the Department, after being informed repeatedly by Congress that the change asked by Postmasters General would not be made, concluded to effect the change by a mere order that would make the statute mean what the practice of sixteen years, and the repeated action of Congress had practically said it did not mean and was never intended to mean. This is a mode of amending and making laws that ought not to be encouraged or approved." This dissent was typical of Justice Harlan. He thought that it was improper thus to burden a publication that put the best literature so cheaply into the hands of the people when there were sufficient constitutional grounds for not doing so.

In the cases of the Standard Oil Company v. United States, 221 U. S. 1, and United States v. American Tobacco Co., 221 U. S. 106, much of the action of the court was not necessary for the decision of the case. Instead of doing the simple thing, the court went out of its way to show that a combination was unreasonable when it could have merely pronounced it in restraint of trade.

When we read Justice Harlan's dissenting opinion from the case of United States v. E. C. Knight Co., 156 U. S. 1, and note how many times he uses the words " unreasonable " and " undue " as modifiers of the phrase " restraint of trade," we wonder why he objected to the use of the words in the Standard Oil decision. On deeper inspection, the reason for this objection becomes evident. If the court had simply said that the restraint was an " unreasonable " restraint of trade without affirmative comment upon the necessity of the word being in the statute, it is doubtful whether Justice Harlan would have dissented at all. It was the manner in which the word was employed that he disliked. The word was added after considerable weighing of the wording of the statute and lengthy investigation into the meaning and methods of regulating monopolies. And it must be further noted that Congress had long remained silent after a dissenting opinion of the same judge had suggested that the word be supplied. This fact argued to Justice Harlan's mind that Congress meant that the word should not be supplied.

The following quotation will show the court's argument in the Standard Oil case: " And as the contracts or acts embraced in the provision were not expressly defined, since the enumeration addressed itself simply to classes of acts, those classes being broad enough to embrace every conceivable contract or combination which could be made concerning trade or commerce or the subjects of such commerce, and thus caused any act done by any of the enumerated methods anywhere in the whole field of human activity to be illegal if in restraint of trade, it inevitably follows that the provision necessarily called for the exercise of judgment which required that some standard should be resorted to for the purpose of determining whether the prohibition contained in the statute had or had not in any given case been violated. Thus not specifying, but indubitably contemplating and requiring a standard, it follows that it was intended that the standard of reason which had been applied at the common law and in this country in dealing with subjects of the character embraced by the statute was intended to be the measure used for the purpose of determining whether, in a given case, a particular act had or had not brought about the wrong against which the statute provided."

As has been seen, Justice Harlan in his dissent in the Standard Oil case first condemned the court for dwelling at length on a point which did not need to be dwelt on in order to decide the case. He then entered upon some generalizations as to the evil effects to be expected by such action on the part of the court. He said: "I said at the outset that the action of the court in this case might well alarm thoughtful men who revered the Constitution. I meant by this that many things are intimated and said in the court's opinion which will not be regarded otherwise than as sanctioning an invasion by the judiciary of the constitutional domain of Congress,—an attempt by interpretation to soften or modify what some regard as a harsh public policy. This court, let me repeat, solemnly adjudged many years ago that it could not, except by '*judicial legislation*,' read words into the anti-trust act not put there by Congress, and which, being inserted, gives it a meaning which the words of the act, as passed, if properly interpreted, would not justify. The court has decided that it could not thus change a public policy formulated and declared by Congress; that Congress has paramount authority to regulate interstate commerce, and that it alone can change a policy once inaugurated by legislation. The courts have nothing to do with the wisdom or policy of an act of Congress. Their duty is to ascertain the will of Congress, and if the statute embodying the expression of that will is constitutional, the courts must respect it. They have no function to declare a public policy, nor to *amend legislative enactments*."

The following assertions may almost be looked upon as parting words from a great judge to his country. "After many years of public service at the national capital, and after a somewhat close observation of the conduct of public affairs, I am impelled to say that there is abroad in our land a most harmful tendency to bring about the amending of constitutions and legislative enactments by means alone of judicial construction. As a public policy has been declared by the legislative department in respect of interstate commerce, over which Congress has entire control, under the Constitution, all concerned must patiently submit to what has been lawfully done, until the people of the United States —the source of all national power—shall, in their own time, upon reflection and through the legislative department of the government, require a change of that policy. . . . The supreme law of the land, which is binding alike upon all,— upon Presidents, Congresses, the courts and the people,— gives to Congress, and to Congress alone, authority to regulate interstate commerce, and when Congress forbids *any* restraint of such commerce, in any form, all must obey its mandate. To overreach the action of Congress merely by judicial construction, that is, by indirection, is a blow at the integrity of our governmental system, and in the end will prove most dangerous to all."

Justice Harlan's Idea of the Position of the Court.—Since the position of judges in the interpretation of laws gives rise to so much discussion, it is well to consider this whole question. An attempt will be made to ascertain how far Justice Harlan's doctrine on this matter came from the position which it is evident that judges ought to occupy. There is much uncertainty on this point in the mind of the public. A person will condemn the court today for not reading into the law a meaning which he desires to see there, and tomorrow he will condemn it more severely for reading into the law a meaning which he did not want to see there. How far, therefore, if at all, should the judges try to meet this public approval or disapproval? Thus is opened up the whole question of judicial legislation.

There are practically two arguments presented, and both are presented on either side of the question. The first, stated affirmatively, is that the very act of interpretation itself implies judicial legislation; stated negatively, it is that interpretation, properly speaking, does not imply judicial legislation. The second argument is that the failure of the court at times to legislate judicially gives rise to adverse criticism and weakens the power of the court. But this same argument is presented on the other side, with a like comment that a continued exercise of judicial legislation may in time even destroy the power of the courts. These conceptions cover practically the whole field.

The word interpret used in a legal sense has two meanings: first, "the setting forth of a fixed or certain meaning, discoverable by a purely intellectual process"; and secondly, the setting forth "of a meaning which is indeterminate or uncertain."[1] The former is called analytical interpretation, and the latter selective interpretation. According to those who uphold judicial legislation, the latter is of far greater importance. It arises when the courts are called upon to decide the bearing of the law upon cases which the legislative did not have in mind when the law was passed. "The fact is that the difficulties of so-called interpretation arise when the Legislature has had no meaning at all; when the question which is raised on the statute never occurred to it; when what the judges have to do is, not to determine what the Legislature did mean on a point which was present to its mind, but to guess what it would have intended on a point not present to its mind, if the point had been present."[2]

Thus the necessity of judicial legislation arises. When unforeseen circumstances come up, and when there is a law in existence which the courts can stretch to apply to such cases, they do it. This is known as selective interpretation, and amounts, in the long run, to judicial legislation, for in the course of time the law may become so much changed that by reading the statute in the light of existing circumstances the original purpose of the law is changed.

Some persons who have observed this necessity have concluded that since the court changes laws it in fact legislates, and it should be frankly admitted that it is the body that

---

[1] Editorial, "Genuine and Spurious Interpretation," in the Green Bag, vol. xxv, p. 505.
[2] J. C. Gray, The Nature and Sources of the Law, Sec. 370.

makes laws. Without going deeply into this matter, the simple assertion will suffice that an open assumption on the part of the courts that they may, when they find it necessary, make laws to suit their purposes would be a dangerous enlargement of the power of the courts. The fact that the judges must argue that what they are doing is not legislating, but only applying laws already made, keeps them from extending their power over any sphere that undoubtedly belongs to the legislature.

On the other hand, when the assertion is made that interpretation properly speaking does not imply judicial legislation, one has in mind especially analytical interpretation—a discovery of the meaning of the law by purely intellectual processes. Strictly speaking, those holding to this theory believe that the law can be made in advance of every case to be determined. All that the courts need to do is to find out the facts in the case and say what the law directs for that case. Their judgment is to be mechanical, and judges are merely experts applying legal formulas to cases, and lose sight of all other considerations.

But this is not the conception that modern jurisconsults hold when they assert that interpretation should not mean judicial legislation. They recognize the fact of legal fictions and the necessity of judge-made law through slow processes, ·but they oppose any quick and intentional change in a statute on the part of the court. In other words, they do not hold that judges should openly and avowedly perform judicial legislation, or that they should underhandedly argue that what is clearly judicial legislation is within the meaning of the statute. They do not object to the slowly evolving judge-made law, developed from necessity. The latter is finding law to meet exigencies, the former is changing the law to suit the convenience of the judge. With them, finding the law is indicative of a great judge, but changing the law is indicative of arrogance.

To which of these classes did Justice Harlan belong? At the outset it must be admitted that there is no evidence that he thought deeply of judicial legislation as a legal concept. His assertions were spontaneous, and if they show him to belong to the class of great judges, it will be all the more in his favor. It will class him as an unconscious artist in that regard.

Reference will need to be made chiefly to the first and last cases studied under the head of judicial legislation. Did the case of United States v. Clark show him to be a great or an inferior judge? No doubt Clark might have suffered hardship had the case been decided according to Justice Harlan's view. But was that hardship one that the judges could properly have remedied? The meaning of the statute was clear. It was evident that if the law applied, Clark's claim would not have been absolved. But since the law on its face was written to exclude such a case, and since it was impossible so to read the statute that it would except him, the law should have been upheld. Congress could have remedied such a situation. There was no excuse for the failure of the court to see in the statute what was really there. And to say the least, this case does not show Justice Harlan to be an inferior judge. It shows loyalty to the Constitution and the firmness necessary in the upholding of the steadiness of the law. Many exceptions of this nature would make the law weak-kneed.

The case of United States v. Clark, however, is rather an exceptional one. There is only one other case,[3] as far as I know, where Justice Harlan opposed leniency to the individual. When it was possible for him to argue that the law allowed relief from hardship, he held to that interpretation. As has been pointed out in various places throughout this study, he practically always endeavored to relieve the suffering individual, but his sense of truth kept him from saying that a law was not what it clearly was. But in the case of the Standard Oil Company v. United States there were none of those exigencies which demanded judicial leniency. Certainly the Standard Oil Company needed

---

[3] United States v. Jung Ah Lung, 124 U. S. 621.

no such protecting care. If there was any real exigency, it was that condition which the phrase "restraint of trade" described. The public feeling which the legislators were seeking to put into law was prompted by the hardship brought upon individuals by the monopolies. If there were any exigencies that demanded leniency they were certainly not on the part of the Standard Oil Company.

Justice Harlan did not stand for the strict letter of the law; he stood for legality. In the case of Louisiana v. Mayor, etc., of New Orleans he showed this by desiring that a judgment against the city be termed a contract. Strict letter said that it was not a contract, but legality said that the city was liable to the plaintiff. This case is typical of many. If the law could be found to cover the case, he believed in deciding that way. But if a law could be found which was expressly different from what the judges wanted it to be, he contended that the latter should hold exactly as it was meant. He believed that Congress should supply the laws, and that the courts should interpret them, and he used interpretation in the liberal sense. He did not wish to stop legal fictions, but he did wish to see judges impartial.

The second argument proposed need not be discussed, except to say that mere criticism of a judicial decision seemed not to be of great concern to Justice Harlan. With him the criticism for bad law had to be thrown on the legislators. Since words have meanings, and since legislators have the power of using words and sentences in their proper relation, he thought that legislators could make laws to fit certain circumstances. If a circumstance arose to which the law applied, it was the duty of the court to apply and enforce the law as the legislators had made it. It must be remembered that the best way to get rid of a bad law is to have it enforced by the courts. Since that is true, Justice Harlan's doctrine that a law should be enforced exactly as the legislators meant it to be enforced is a sound one.

INDEX

American Sugar Refining Company, 92.
American Tobacco Company, 99.
Amount in dispute,—relation to jurisdiction of courts, 168–172.

Bailey, Joseph W., 15 (note).
Beckham, candidate for Lieut. Gov. of Ky., 74, 75.
Behring Sea Tribunal, 11.
Berea College, Kentucky, 126, 136–137.
Bowdoin College, 10.
Bradley, William, 12 (note).
Brewer, Justice, 90.
Bristow, General B. H., 10.
Brown, Justice, 117, 185.

Centre College, Kentucky, 10.
Chinese, discrimination against, 137–141.
Cincinnati, Republican convention at, 10.
Contracts,—freedom of in interstate commerce, 114–121.
Contracts,—relation of foreign governments to, 55–58.
Contracts,—relation of national government to, 52–55.
Contracts,—relation of state governments to, 43–52.
Copyrights, 182–183.
Corporations,—as citizens, 143.
Corporations,—taxation of, 145–152.
Corporations,—under equal protection of laws, 142–152.

Direct taxes, 176–180.
Drummers, taxation of, 103–105.
Due Process of Law,—definition of, 59–61.
Due Process of Law,—relation to life and liberty, 61–68.
Due Process of Law,—relation to property, 68–82.

Employers' Liability, 121–122.
Equity competence, 166–168.
Esterling, Blackburn, 13 (note).
Exports, taxation of, 107–112.
Ex post facto laws, 180–182.

Federal immunity, 161–166.
Field, Justice, 13, 69, 140, 173.
Fourteenth Amendment,—bearing upon first eight, 173–176.
Franchises,—taxation of, 106–107.
Fuller, Justice, 113, 185.

George Washington University, 10.
Goebel,—candidate for governorship of Kentucky, 74, 75.
Gray, Justice, 39, 87, 108.
Gray's Nature and Sources of the Law, 203 (note).
Greenbag, 203 (note).
Gross railroad receipts,—taxation of, 112–114.

Harlan, the Hon. James S., 10.
Harlan, Mr. John Maynard, 10.
Harlan, Dr. R. D., 10.
Hayes, R. B.—appoints Justice Harlan to Supreme Court, 12.
Hayes, R. B.—Republican nominee of Cincinnati Convention, 10.
Holmes, Justice, 40, 112, 122, 164, 170, 183.
Houghton, Mifflin and Co., 198.

Indians,—discrimination against, 141–143.
Infantry, Tenth Kentucky, 9.
Insular Cases, 185–188.
Interstate comity, 188–190.
Interstate Commerce Commission, beginning of, 122–125.

Jim crow laws, 89–92, 126, 132–134.

207

9 7 8 1 5 8 4 7 7 4 4 6 4